Virtues

of

Friendship and Loyalty

WILLIAM J. BENNETT

W PUBLISHING GROUP™

www.wpublishinggroup.com

A Division of Thomas Nelson, Inc.
www.ThomasNelson.com

Published by W Publishing Group, a Division of Thomas Nelson, Inc., P.O. Box 141000, Nashville,
Tennessee 37214.

Material in this book is compiled from both *The Book of Virtues* and *The Moral Compass* by William
J. Bennett, copyright © 1993 by William J. Bennett and copyright © 1996 by William J. Bennett.

Published by arrangement with Simon & Schuster, Inc.

Library of Congress Cataloging-in-Publication Data

Virtues of friendship and loyalty / [edited by] William J. Bennett.
    p. cm.
  ISBN 0-8499-1725-5
  1. Friendship—Literary collections. I. Bennett, William J. (William John), 1943–
PN6071.D7 V57 2001
808.8'0353—dc21   2001046970

Printed in the United States of America

01 02 03 04 05 BVG 5 4 3 2 1

Contents

Introduction

WILLIAM J. BENNETT

Everyone wants friends. They make us happy. They make life interesting and fun and profitable for us. They share our tastes, our desires, our sense of humor. And on a deeper level, friends help us become better human beings. The virtues demanded in real friendship—qualities such as honesty, trust, kindness, and generosity—all help us grow in a moral sense. The best of friends try to make each other better people. They lift each other up.

Of course, there are bad friendships too, the kind of relationships the English essayist Joseph Addison called "confederacies in vice, or leagues of pleasure." Our desires and selfishness can be the foundation of counterfeit friendships that pull us down. And that is exactly why picking friends is among the most important decisions we make in life. In our age, when casual intimacy comes so quickly and cheaply, we need to remember that friends are supposed to help protect us from our weaknesses, not help us indulge them. As we read in Ecclesiasticus, "A faithful friend is a strong defense: and he that hath found such an one hath found a treasure."

The Greek philosopher Aristotle summed up friendship this way: "We may describe friendly feeling toward anyone as wishing for him what you believe to be good things, not for your own sake but for his, and being inclined, so far as you can, to bring these things about." That means thinking not so much about *having* friends as *being* a good friend. It means friendship is based, in no small degree, on giving.

One of the most important things we give in any friendship is our loyalty, a trait that sometimes seems as though it needs to be placed on an endangered virtues list. Loyalty to family, to country, to community, to one's company—we should not regard these as quaint, outmoded notions. In an age when people are told to "do what feels good" and "do your own thing," the idea of loyalty reminds us that often we should be ready to look past our own needs and put someone or something else first. Loyalty, at bottom, means self-sacrifice, the kind of self-sacrifice that gives solid meaning to relationships.

Our loyalties, like our friendships, are important signs of the kinds of persons we have chosen to become. They mark a steadfastness in our attachments to other people, groups, institutions, or ideals. To be a loyal citizen or friend means to operate within a certain framework of caring seriously about the well-being of one's country or comrade. Real loyalty endures inconvenience, withstands temptation, and does not cringe under assault. The trust that genuine loyalty generates can pervade our whole lives.

These two virtues, friendship and loyalty, are deep things. They both take effort to develop and work to keep. They are necessary virtues for a good life.

Aristotle on Friendship

From *The Nicomachean Ethics*

The ancients listed friendship among the highest of virtues. It was an essential element in the happy or fully flourishing life. "For without friends," Aristotle says, "no one would choose to live, though he had all other goods." Words worth remembering in a world of perishable "goods."

According to Aristotle, friendship either is, or it involves, a state of character, a virtue. There are three kinds of friendship. These are based on pleasure in another's company (friendships of pleasure), or on usefulness in association (friendships of utility), or on mutual admiration (friendships in virtue). All are essential to the good life, and the best sorts of friends will not only admire each other's excellence but take pleasure in each other's company and find their association of mutual advantage. Here is a portion of Aristotle's classic discussion.

A s the motives to Friendship differ in kind, so do the respective feelings and Friendships. The species then of Friendship are three, in number equal to the objects of it, since in the line of each there may be "mutual affection mutually known."

Now they who have Friendship for one another desire one another's good according to the motive of their Friendship; accordingly they whose motive is utility have no Friendship for one another really, but only insofar as some good arises to them from one another.

And they whose motive is pleasure are in like case: I mean, they have Friendship for men of easy pleasantry, not because they are of a given character but because they are pleasant to themselves. So then they whose motive to Friendship is utility love their friends for what is good to themselves; they whose motive is pleasure do so for what is pleasurable to themselves; that is to say, not insofar as the friend beloved *is* but insofar as he is useful or pleasurable. These Friendships then are a matter of result: since the object is not beloved in that he is the man he is but in that he furnishes advantage or pleasure as the case may be.

Such Friendships are, of course, very liable to dissolution if the parties do not continue alike: I mean, that the others cease to have any Friendship for them when they are no longer pleasurable or useful. Now it is the nature of utility not to be permanent but constantly varying: so, of course, when the motive which made them friends is vanished, the Friendship likewise dissolves; since it existed only relatively to those circumstances. . . .

That then is perfect Friendship which subsists between those who are good and whose similarity consists in their goodness: for these men wish one another's good in similar ways; insofar as they are good (and good they are in themselves); and those are specially friends who wish good to their friends for their sakes, because they feel thus toward them on their own account and not as a mere matter of result; so the Friendship between these men continues to subsist so long as they are good; and goodness, we know, has in it a principle of permanence. . . .

Rare it is probable Friendships of this kind will be, because men of this kind are rare. Besides, all requisite qualifications being presupposed, there is further required time and intimacy: for, as the proverb says, men cannot know one another "till they have eaten the requisite quantity of salt together"; nor can they in fact admit one another to intimacy, much less be friends, till each has appeared to the other and been proved to be a fit object of Friendship. They who speedily commence an interchange of friendly actions may be said to wish to be friends, but they are not so unless they are also proper objects of Friendship and mutually known to be such: that is to say, a desire for Friendship may arise quickly but not Friendship itself.

Baucis and Philemon

RETOLD BY THOMAS BULFINCH

The ancient Greeks understood that the health of the community depended on how well its individual citizens treated one another. To them, Zeus, the king of the gods, was both the guardian of the state and the protector of human relations among civilized men. All social institutions, including the family, lay in his care. Travelers in particular honored him, for he rewarded those who remembered the rules of hospitality and duties of friendship, as we see in this story in which Zeus and Hermes (Jupiter and Mercury to the Romans) seek shelter among the mortals.

Once upon a time Jupiter, in human shape, visited the land of Phrygia, and with him Mercury, without his wings. They presented themselves as weary travelers at many a door, seeking rest and shelter, but found all closed; for it was late, and the inhospitable inhabitants would not rouse themselves to open for their reception. At last a small thatched cottage received them, where Baucis, a pious old dame, and her husband, Philemon, had grown old together. Not ashamed of their poverty, they made it endurable by moderate desires and kind dispositions. When the two guests crossed the humble threshold and bowed their heads to pass under the low door, the old man placed a seat, on which Baucis, bustling and attentive, spread a cloth, and begged them to sit down. Then she raked out the coals from the ashes, kindled a fire, and prepared some pot-herbs and bacon for them. A beechen bowl was filled with warm water, that their guests might wash. While all was doing, they beguiled the time with conversation.

The old woman with trembling hand set the table. One leg was shorter than the rest, but a piece of slate put under restored the level. When it was steady she rubbed the table down with sweet-smelling herbs. Upon it she set some of chaste Minerva's olives, some cornel berries preserved in vinegar, and added radishes and cheese, with eggs lightly cooked in the ashes. The meal was served in earthen dishes; and an earthenware pitcher, with wooden cups, stood beside them. When all was ready, the stew, smoking hot, was set on the table. Some wine, not of the oldest, was added, and for dessert, apples and wild honey.

Now while the repast proceeded, the old folks were astonished to see that the wine, as fast as it was poured out, renewed itself in the pitcher of its own accord. Struck with terror, Baucis and Philemon recognized their heavenly guests, fell on their knees, and with clasped hands implored forgiveness for their poor entertainment. There was an old goose, which they kept as the guardian of their humble cottage, and they bethought them to make this a sacrifice in honor of their guests. But the goose, too nimble for the old folk, with the aid of feet and wings eluded their pursuit and at last took shelter between the gods themselves. They forbade it to be slain and spoke in these words: "We are gods. This inhospitable village shall pay the penalty of its impiety; you alone shall go free from the chastisement. Quit your house and come with us to the top of yonder hill." They hastened to obey. The country behind them was speedily sunk in a lake, only their own house left standing. While they gazed with wonder at the sight, that old house of theirs was changed. Columns took the place of the corner posts, the thatch grew yellow and appeared a gilded roof, the floors became marble, the doors were enriched with carving and ornaments of gold. Then spoke Jupiter in benign accents: "Excellent old man, and woman worthy of such a husband, speak, tell us your wishes. What favor have you to ask of us?" Philemon took counsel with Baucis a few moments, then declared to the gods their common wish. "We ask to be priests and guardians of this thy temple, and that one and the same hour may take us both from life." Their prayer was granted. When they had attained a great age, as they stood one day before the steps of the sacred edifice and were telling the story of the place, Baucis saw Philemon begin to put forth leaves, and Philemon saw Baucis changing in like manner. While still they exchanged parting words, a leafy crown grew over their heads. "Farewell, dear spouse," they said together, and at the same moment the bark closed over their mouths. The Tyanean shepherd still shows the two trees—an oak and a linden, standing side by side.

Cat and Mouse in Partnership

THE BROTHERS GRIMM

As this story shows us, picking the wrong friend can be disappointing or even disastrous.

A cat having made acquaintance with a mouse, professed such great love and friendship for her that the mouse at last agreed that they should live and keep house together.

"We must make provision for the winter," said the cat, "or we shall suffer hunger, and you, little mouse, must not stir out, or you will be caught in a trap."

So they took counsel together and bought a little pot of honey. And then they could not tell where to put it for safety, but after long consideration, the cat said there could not be a better place than the church, for nobody would steal there, and they would put it under the altar and not touch it until they were really in want. So this was done, and the little pot placed in safety.

But before long the cat was seized with a great wish to taste it.

"Listen to me, little mouse," said he. "I have been asked by my cousin to stand godfather to a little son she has brought into the world. He is white with brown spots. And they want to have the christening today, so let me go to it, and you stay at home and keep house."

"Oh, yes, certainly," answered the mouse. "Pray go by all means. And when you are feasting on all the good things, think of me. I should so like a drop of the sweet red wine."

But there was not a word of truth in all this. The cat had no cousin, and had not been asked to stand godfather. He went to the church, straight up to the little pot, and licked the honey off the top. Then he took a walk over the roofs of the town, saw his acquaintances, stretched himself in the sun, and licked his whiskers as often as he thought of the little pot of honey. And then when it was evening he went home.

"Here you are at last," said the mouse. "I expect you have had a merry time."

"Oh, pretty well," answered the cat.

"And what name did you give the child?" asked the mouse.

"Top-off," answered the cat, dryly.

"Top-off!" cried the mouse. "That is a singular and wonderful name! Is it common in your family?"

"What does it matter?" said the cat. "It's not any worse than Crumb-picker, like your godchild."

A little time after this the cat was again seized with a longing.

"Again I must ask you," said he to the mouse, "to do me a favor, and keep house alone for a day. I have been asked a second time to stand godfather. And as the little one has a white ring around its neck, I cannot well refuse."

So the kind little mouse consented, and the cat crept along by the town wall until he reached the church, and going straight to the little pot of honey, devoured half of it.

"Nothing tastes so well as what one keeps to oneself," said he, feeling quite content with his day's work. When he reached home, the mouse asked what name had been given to the child.

"Half-gone," answered the cat.

"Half-gone!" cried the mouse. "I never heard such a name in my life! I'll bet it's not to be found in the calendar."

Soon after that the cat's mouth began to water again for the honey.

"Good things always come in threes," said he to the mouse. "Again I have been asked to stand godfather; the little one is quite black with white feet, and not any white hair on its body. Such a thing does not happen every day, so you will let me go, won't you?"

"Top-off, Half-gone," murmured the mouse. "They are such curious names, I cannot but wonder at them!"

"That's because you are always sitting at home," said the cat, "in your little gray frock and hairy tail, never seeing the world, and fancying all sorts of things."

So the little mouse cleaned up the house and set it all in order. Meanwhile the greedy cat went and made an end of the little pot of honey.

"Now that all is finished, one's mind will be easy," said he, and came home in the evening, quite sleek and comfortable. The mouse asked at once what name had been given to the third child.

"It won't please you any better than the others," answered the cat. "It is called All-gone."

"All-gone!" cried the mouse. "What an unheard-of name! I never met with anything like it! All-gone! Whatever can it mean?" And shaking her head, she curled herself round and went to sleep. After that the cat was not again asked to stand godfather.

When the winter had come and there was nothing more to be had out of doors, the mouse began to think of their store.

"Come, cat," said she, "we will fetch our pot of honey; how good it will taste, to be sure!"

"Of course, it will," said the cat.

So they set out, and when they reached the place, they found the pot, but it was standing empty.

"Oh, now I know what it all meant," cried the mouse. "Now I see what sort of a partner you have been! Instead of standing godfather you have devoured it all, first Top-off, then Half-gone, then—"

"Will you hold your tongue!" screamed the cat. "Another word, and I'll devour you, too!"

And the poor little mouse having "All-gone" on her tongue, out it came, and the cat leaped upon her and made an end of her. And that is the way of the world.

The Child's Story

CHARLES DICKENS

What are we here for, if not to walk with each other along life's journey?

Once upon a time, a good many years ago, there was a traveler, and he set out upon a journey. It was a magic journey, and seemed very long when he began it, and very short when he got halfway through.

He traveled along a rather dark path for some little time, without meeting anything, until at last he came to a beautiful child. So he said to the child, "What do you do here?" And the child said, "I am always at play. Come and play with me!"

So he played with that child, the whole day long, and they were very merry. The sky was so blue, and the sun was so bright, the water was so sparkling, the leaves were so green, the flowers were so lovely, and they heard such singing birds and saw so many butterflies, that everything was beautiful. This was in fine weather. When it rained, they loved to watch the falling drops, and to smell the fresh scents. When it blew, it was delightful to listen to the wind, and fancy what it said as it came rushing from its home—where was that, they wondered!—whistling and howling, driving the clouds before it, bending the trees, rumbling in the chimneys, shaking the house, and making the sea roar in fury. But when it snowed, that was best of all, for they liked nothing so well as to look up at the white flakes falling fast and thick, like down from the breasts of millions of white birds, and to see how smooth and deep the drift was, and to listen to the hush upon the paths and roads.

They had plenty of the finest toys in the world, and the most astonishing picture books—all about scimitars and slippers and turbans, and dwarfs and giants and genii and fairies, and Bluebeards and beanstalks and riches and caverns and forests and Valentines and Orsons—and all new and all true.

But one day, of a sudden, the traveler lost the child. He called to him over and over again, but got no answer. So he went upon his road, and went on for a little while without meeting anything, until at last he came to a handsome boy. So he said to the boy, "What do you do here?" And the boy said, "I am always learning. Come and learn with me."

So he learned with that boy about Jupiter and Juno, and the Greeks and the Romans, and I don't know what, and learned more than I could tell—or he, either, for he soon forgot a great deal of it. But they were not always learning; they had the merriest games that ever were played. They rowed upon the river in summer, and skated on the ice in winter; they were active afoot, and active on horseback, at cricket, and all games at ball; at prisoner's base, hare and hounds, follow my leader, and more sports than I can think of. Nobody could beat them. They had holidays, too, the Twelfth Night cakes, and parties where they danced till midnight, and real theaters where they saw palaces of real gold and silver rise out of the real earth, and saw all the wonders of the world at once. As to friends, they had such dear friends and so many of them that I want time to reckon them up. They were all young, like the handsome boy, and were never to be strange to one another all their lives through.

Still, one day, in the midst of all these pleasures, the traveler lost the boy as he had lost the child, and, after calling to him in vain, went on upon his journey. So he went on for a little while without seeing anything, until at last he came to a young man. So he said to the young man, "What do you do here?" And the young man said, "I am always in love. Come and love with me."

So he went with that young man, and presently they came to one of the prettiest girls that was ever seen—just like Fanny in the corner there—and she had eyes like Fanny, and hair like Fanny, and dimples like Fanny, and she laughed and colored just as Fanny does while I am talking about her. So the young man fell in love directly—just as Somebody I won't mention, the first time he came here, did with Fanny. Well! He was teased sometimes—just as Somebody used to be by Fanny; and they quarreled sometimes—just as Somebody and Fanny used to quarrel; and they made it up, and sat in the dark, and wrote letters every day, and never were happy asunder, and were always looking out for each other and pretending not to, and were engaged at

Christmastime, and sat close to each other by the fire, and were going to be married very soon—all exactly like Somebody I won't mention, and Fanny!

But the traveler lost them one day, as he had lost the rest of his friends, and, after calling to them to come back, which they never did, went on upon his journey. So he went on for a little while without seeing anything, until at last he came to a middle-aged gentleman. So he said to the gentleman, "What are you doing here?" And his answer was, "I am always busy. Come and be busy with me!"

So he began to be very busy with that gentleman, and they went on through the wood together. The whole journey was through a wood, only it had been open and green at first, like a wood in spring, and now began to be thick and dark, like a wood in summer. Some of the little trees that had come out earliest were even turning brown. The gentleman was not alone, but had a lady of about the same age with him, who was his wife; and they had children, who were with them, too. So they all went on together through the wood, cutting down the trees, and making a path through the branches and the fallen leaves, and carrying burdens and working hard.

Sometimes they came to a long green avenue that opened into deeper woods. Then they would hear a very little distant voice crying: "Father, Father, I am another child! Stop for me!" And presently they would see a very little figure, growing larger as it came along, running to join them. When it came up, they all crowded around it, and kissed and welcomed it; and then they all went on together.

Sometimes they came to several avenues at once, and then they all stood still, and one of the children said, "Father, I am going to sea," and another said, "Father, I am going to India," and another, "Father, I am going to seek my fortune where I can," and another, "Father, I am going to Heaven!" So, with many tears at parting, they went, solitary, down those avenues, each child upon its way; and the child who went to Heaven rose into the golden air and vanished.

Whenever these partings happened, the traveler looked at the gentleman and saw him glance up at the sky above the trees, where the day was beginning to decline, and the sunset to come on. He saw, too, that his hair was turning gray. But they never could rest long, for they had their journey to perform, and it was necessary for them to be always busy.

At last, there had been so many partings that there were no children left, and only the traveler, the gentleman, and the lady went upon their way in company. And now the wood was yellow; and now brown; and the leaves, even of the forest trees, began to fall. They came to an avenue that was darker than the rest, and were pressing forward on their journey without looking down it when the lady stopped.

"My husband," said the lady, "I am called."

They listened, and they heard a voice, a long way down the avenue, say, "Mother, Mother!"

It was the voice of the first child who had said, "I am going to Heaven!" and the father said: "I pray not yet. The sunset is very near. I pray not yet!"

But the voice cried, "Mother, Mother!" without minding him,

though his hair was now quite white, and tears were on his face.

Then the mother, who was already drawn into the shade of the dark avenue and moving away with her arms still around his neck, kissed him, and said, "My dearest, I am summoned, and I go!" And she was gone. And the traveler and he were left alone together.

And they went on and on together, until they came to very near the end of the wood; so near that they could see the sunset shining red before them through the trees.

Yet once more, while he broke his way among the branches, the traveler lost his friend. He called and called, but there was no reply, and when he passed out of the wood, and saw the peaceful sun going down upon a wide purple prospect, he came to an old man sitting on a fallen tree. So he said to the old man, "What do you do here?" And the old man said with a calm smile: "I am always remembering. Come and remember with me!"

So the traveler sat down by the side of that old man, face to face with the serene sunset; and all his friends came softly back and stood around him. The beautiful child, the handsome boy, the young man in love, the father, the mother, and the children: every one of them was there, and he had lost nothing. So he loved them all, and was kind and forbearing with them all, and was always pleased to watch them all, and they all honored and loved him. And I think the traveler must be yourself, dear Grandfather, because this is what you do to us, and what we do to you.

Damon and Pythias

TRADITIONAL

This story takes place in the Sicilian city-state of Syracuse in the fourth century B.C. The Roman orator Cicero tells us that Damon and Pythias (also called Phintias) were followers of the philosopher Pythagoras. Even today, their story sets the standard for absolute friendship, which gives every reason for confidence and leaves no room for doubts.

Damon and Pythias had been the best of friends since childhood. Each trusted the other like a brother, and each knew in his heart there was nothing he would not do for his friend. Eventually the time came for them to prove the depth of their devotion. It happened this way.

Dionysius, the ruler of Syracuse, grew annoyed when he heard about the kind of speeches Pythias was giving. The young scholar was telling the public that no man should have unlimited power over another, and that absolute tyrants were unjust kings. In a fit of rage, Dionysius summoned Pythias and his friend.

"Who do you think you are, spreading unrest among the people?" he demanded.

"I spread only the truth," Pythias answered. "There can be nothing wrong with that."

"And does your truth hold that kings have too much power and that their laws are not good for their subjects?"

"If a king has seized power without permission of the people, then that is what I say."

"This kind of talk is treason," Dionysius shouted. "You are conspiring to overthrow me. Retract what you've said, or face the consequences."

"I will retract nothing," Pythias answered.

"Then you will die. Do you have any last requests?"

"Yes. Let me go home just long enough to say good-bye to my wife and children and to put my household in order."

"I see you not only think I'm unjust, you think I'm stupid as well," Dionysius laughed scornfully. "If I let you leave Syracuse, I have no doubt I will never see you again."

"I will give you a pledge," Pythias said.

"What kind of pledge could you possibly give to make me think you will ever return?" Dionysius demanded.

At that instant Damon, who had stood quietly beside his friend, stepped forward.

"I will be his pledge," he said. "Keep me here in Syracuse, as your prisoner, until Pythias returns. Our friendship is well known to you. You can be sure Pythias will return so long as you hold me."

Dionysius studied the two friends silently. "Very well," he said at last. "But if you are willing to take the place of your friend, you must be willing to accept his sentence if he breaks his promise. If Pythias does not return to Syracuse, you will die in his place."

"He will keep his word," Damon replied. "I have no doubt of that."

Pythias was allowed to go free for a time, and Damon was thrown into prison. After several days, when Pythias failed to reappear, Dionysius's curiosity got the better of him, and he went to the prison to see if Damon was yet sorry he had made such a bargain.

"Your time is almost up," the ruler of Syracuse sneered. "It will be useless to beg for mercy. You were a fool to rely on your friend's promise. Did you really think he would sacrifice his life for you or anyone else?"

"He has merely been delayed," Damon answered steadily. "The winds have kept him from sailing, or perhaps he has met with some accident on the road. But if it is humanly possible, he will be here on time. I am as confident of his virtue as I am of my own existence."

Dionysius was startled at the prisoner's confidence. "We shall soon see," he said, and left Damon in his cell.

The fatal day arrived. Damon was brought from prison and led before the executioner. Dionysius greeted him with a smug smile. "It seems your friend has not turned up," he laughed. "What do you think of him now?"

"He is my friend," Damon answered. "I trust him."

Even as he spoke, the doors flew open, and Pythias staggered into the room. He was pale and bruised and half speechless from exhaustion. He rushed to the arms of his friend.

"You are safe, praise the gods," he gasped. "It seemed as though the fates were conspiring against us. My ship was wrecked in a storm, then bandits attacked me on the road. But I refused to give up hope, and at last I've made it back in time. I am ready to receive my sentence of death."

Dionysius heard his words with astonishment. His eyes and his heart were opened. It was impossible for him to resist the power of such constancy.

"The sentence is revoked," he declared. "I never believed that such faith and loyalty could exist in friendship. You have shown me how wrong I was, and it is only right that you be rewarded with your freedom. But I ask that in return you do me one great service."

"What service do you mean?" the friends asked.

"Teach me how to be part of so worthy a friendship."

The Devoted Friend

O S C A R   W I L D E

Devotion is a two-way street between friends, as this Oscar Wilde story reminds us.

One morning the old Water Rat put his head out of his hole. He had bright beady eyes and stiff gray whiskers, and his tail was like a long bit of black India rubber. The little ducks were swimming about in the pond, looking just like a lot of yellow canaries, and their mother, who was pure white with real red legs, was trying to teach them how to stand on their heads in the water.

"You will never be in the best society unless you can stand on your heads," she kept saying to them, and every now and then she showed them how it was done. But the little ducks paid no attention to her. They were so young that they did not know what an advantage it is to be in society at all.

"What disobedient children!" cried the old Water Rat. "They really deserve to be drowned."

"Nothing of the kind," answered the Duck. "Everyone must make a beginning, and parents cannot be too patient."

"Ah! I know nothing about the feelings of parents," said the Water Rat. "I am not a family man. In fact, I have never been married, and I never intend to be. Love is all very well in its way, but friendship is much higher. Indeed, I know of nothing in the world that is either nobler or rarer than a devoted friendship."

"And what, pray, is your idea of the duties of a devoted friend?" asked a green Linnet, who was sitting in a willow tree near by, and had overheard the conversation.

"Yes, that is just what I want to know," said the Duck, and she swam away to the end of the pond, and stood upon her head, in order to give her children a good example.

"What a silly question!" cried the Water Rat. "I should expect my devoted friend to be devoted to me, of course."

"And what would you do in return?" said the little bird, swinging upon a silver spray, and flapping his tiny wings.

"I don't understand you," answered the Water Rat.

"Let me tell you a story on the subject," said the Linnet.

"Is the story about me?" asked the Water Rat. "If so, I will listen to it, for I am extremely fond of fiction."

"It is applicable to you," answered the Linnet. And he flew down, and alighting upon the bank, he told the story of "The Devoted Friend."

"Once upon a time," said the Linnet, "there was an honest little fellow named Hans."

"Was he very distinguished?" asked the Water Rat.

"No," answered the Linnet. "I don't think he was distinguished at all, except for his kind heart, and his funny round good-humored face. He lived in a tiny cottage all by himself, and every day he worked in his garden. In all the countryside there was no garden so lovely as his. Sweet William grew there, and gillyflowers, and shepherds' purses, and fair maids of France. There were damask roses, and yellow roses, lilac crocuses, and gold, purple violets and white. Columbine and ladysmock, marjoram and wild basil, the cowslip and the fleur-de-lis, the daffodil and the clove pink bloomed or blossomed in their proper order as the months went by, one flower taking another flower's place, so that there were always beautiful things to look at, and pleasant odors to smell.

"Little Hans had a great many friends, but the most devoted friend of all was big Hugh the Miller. Indeed, so devoted was the rich Miller to little Hans that he would never go by his garden without leaning over the wall and plucking a large nosegay, or a handful of sweet herbs, or filling his pockets with plums and cherries if it was the fruit season.

"'Real friends should have everything in common,' the Miller used to say, and little Hans nodded and smiled, and felt very proud of having a friend with such noble ideas.

"Sometimes, indeed, the neighbors thought it strange that the rich Miller never gave little Hans anything in return, though he had a hundred sacks of flour stored away in his mill, and six milch cows, and a large flock of woolly sheep; but Hans never troubled his head about these things, and nothing gave him greater pleasure than to listen to all the wonderful things the Miller used to say about the unselfishness of true friendship.

"So little Hans worked away in his garden. During the spring, the summer, and the autumn he was very happy, but when the winter came, and he had no fruit or flowers to bring to the market, he suffered a good deal from cold and hunger, and often had to go to bed without any supper but a few dried pears or some hard nuts. In the winter, also, he was extremely lonely, as the Miller never came to see him then.

"'There is no good in my going to see little Hans as long as the snow lasts,' the Miller used to say to his Wife, 'for when people are in trouble they should be left alone, and not be bothered by visitors. That at least is my idea about friendship, and I am sure I am right. So I shall wait till the spring comes, and then I shall pay him a visit, and he will be able to give me a large basket of primroses, and that will make him so happy.'

"'You are certainly very thoughtful about others,' answered the Wife, as she sat in her comfortable armchair by the big pinewood fire. 'Very thoughtful indeed. It is quite a treat to hear you talk about friendship. I am sure the clergyman himself could not say such beautiful things as you do, though he does live in a three-storied house, and wear a gold ring on his little finger.'

"'But could we not ask little Hans up here?' said the Miller's youngest son. 'If poor Hans is in trouble I will give him half my porridge, and show him my white rabbits.'

"'What a silly boy you are!' cried the Miller. 'I really don't know what is the use of sending you to school. You seem not to learn anything. Why, if little Hans came up here, and saw our warm fire, and our good supper, and our great cask of red wine, he might get envious, and envy is a most terrible thing, and would spoil anybody's nature. I certainly will not allow Hans's nature to be spoiled. I am his best friend, and I will always watch over him, and see that he is not led into any temptations. Besides, if Hans came here, he might ask me to let him have some flour on credit, and that I could not do. Flour is one thing, and friendship is another, and they should not be confused. Why, the words are spelt differently, and mean quite different things. Everybody can see that.'

"'How well you talk!' said the Miller's Wife, pouring herself out a large glass of warm ale. 'Really I feel quite drowsy. It is just like being in church.'

"'Lots of people act well,' answered the Miller, 'but very few people talk well, which shows that talking is much the more difficult thing of the two, and much the finer thing also.' And he looked sternly across the table at his little son, who felt so ashamed of himself that he hung his head down, and grew quite scarlet, and began to cry into his tea. However, he was so young that you must excuse him."

"Is that the end of the story?" asked the Water Rat.

"Certainly not," answered the Linnet. "That is the beginning."

"Then you are quite behind the age," said the Water Rat. "Every good storyteller nowadays starts with the end, and then goes on to the beginning, and concludes with the middle. That is the new method. I heard all about it the other day from a critic who was walking round the pond with a young man. He spoke of the matter at great length, and I am sure he must have been right, for he had blue spectacles and a bald head, and whenever the young man made any remark, he always answered 'Pooh!' But pray go on with your story. I like the Miller immensely. I have all kinds of beautiful sentiments myself, so there is a great sympathy between us."

"Well," said the Linnet, hopping now on one leg and now on the other, "as soon as the winter was over, and the primroses began to open their pale yellow stars, the Miller said to his Wife that he would go down and see little Hans.

"'Why, what a good heart you have!' cried his Wife. 'You are always thinking of others. And mind you take the big basket with you for the flowers.'

"So the Miller tied the sails of the windmill together with a strong iron chain, and went down the hill with the basket on his arm.

"'Good morning, little Hans,' said the Miller.

"'Good morning,' said Hans, leaning on his spade, and smiling from ear to ear.

"'And how have you been all the winter?' said the Miller.

"'Well, really,' cried Hans, 'it is very good of you to ask, very good indeed. I am afraid I had rather a hard time of it, but now the spring has come, and I am quite happy, and all my flowers are doing well.'

"'We often talked of you during the winter, Hans,' said the Miller, 'and wondered how you were getting on.'

"'That was kind of you,' said Hans. 'I was half afraid you had forgotten me.'

"'Hans, I am surprised at you,' said the Miller. 'Friendship never forgets. That is the wonderful thing about it, but I am afraid you don't understand the poetry of life. How lovely your primroses are looking, by the by!'

"'They are certainly very lovely,' said Hans, 'and it is a most lucky thing for me that I have so many. I am going to bring them into the market and sell them to the Burgomaster's daughter, and buy back my wheelbarrow with the money.'

"'Buy back your wheelbarrow? You don't mean to say you have sold it? What a very stupid thing to do!'

"'Well, the fact is,' said Hans, 'that I was obliged to. You see the winter was a very bad time for me, and I really had no money at all to buy bread with. So I first sold the silver buttons off my Sunday coat, and then I sold my silver chain, and then I sold my big pipe, and at last I sold my wheelbarrow. But I am going to buy them all back again now.'

"'Hans,' said the Miller, 'I will give you my wheelbarrow. It is not in very good repair. Indeed, one side is gone, and there is something wrong with the wheel spokes. But in spite of that I will give it to you. I know it is very generous of me, and a great many people would think me extremely foolish for parting with it, but I am not like the rest of the world. I think that generosity is the essence of friendship, and, besides, I have got a new wheelbarrow for myself. Yes, you may set your mind at ease. I will give you my wheelbarrow.'

"'Well, really, that is generous of you,' said little Hans, and his funny round face glowed all over with pleasure. 'I can easily put it in repair, as I have a plank of wood in the house.'

"'A plank of wood!' said the Miller. 'Why, that is just what I want for the roof of my barn. There is a very large hole in it, and the corn will all get damp if I don't stop it up. How lucky you mentioned it! It is quite remarkable how one good action always breeds another. I have given you my wheelbarrow, and now you are going to give me your plank. Of course, the wheelbarrow is worth far more than the plank, but true friendship never notices things like that. Pray get it at once, and I will set to work at my barn this very day.'

"'Certainly,' cried little Hans, and he ran into the shed and dragged the plank out.

"'It is not a very big plank,' said the Miller, looking at it, 'and I am afraid that after I have mended my barn roof there won't be any left for you to mend the wheelbarrow with. But, of course, that is not my fault. And now, as I have given you my wheel-barrow, I am sure you would like to give me some flowers in return. Here is the basket, and mind you fill it quite full.'

"'Quite full?' said little Hans, rather sorrowfully, for it was really a very big basket, and he knew that if he filled it he would have no flowers left for the market, and he was very anxious to get his silver buttons back.

"'Well, really,' answered the Miller, 'as I have given you my wheelbarrow, I don't think that it is much to ask you for a few flowers. I may be wrong, but I should have thought that friend-ship, true friendship, was quite free from selfishness of any kind.'

"'My dear friend, my best friend,' cried little Hans, 'you are welcome to all the flowers in my garden. I would much sooner have your good opinion than my silver buttons, any day.' And he ran and plucked all his pretty primroses, and filled the Miller's basket.

"'Goodbye, little Hans,' said the Miller, as he went up the hill with the plank on his shoulder and the big basket in his hand.

"'Goodbye,' said little Hans, and he began to dig away quite merrily, he was so pleased about the wheelbarrow.

"The next day he was nailing up some honeysuckle against the porch, when he heard the Miller's voice calling to him from the road. So he jumped off the ladder, and ran down the garden, and looked over the wall.

"There was the Miller with a large sack of flour on his back.

"'Dear little Hans,' said the Miller, 'would you mind carrying this sack of flour for me to market?'

"'Oh, I am so sorry,' said Hans, 'but I am really very busy today. I have got all my creepers to nail up, and all my flowers to water, and all my grass to roll.'

"'Well, really,' said the Miller. 'I think that, considering that I am going to give you my wheelbarrow, it is rather unfriendly of you to refuse.'

"'Oh, don't say that,' cried little Hans. 'I wouldn't be unfriendly for the whole world.' And he ran in for his cap, and trudged off with the big sack on his shoulders.

"It was a very hot day, and the road was terribly dusty, and before Hans had reached the sixth milestone he was so tired that he had to sit down and rest. However, he went on bravely, and at last he reached the market. After he had waited there some time, he sold the sack of flour for a very good price, and then he returned home at once, for he was afraid that if he stopped too late he might meet some robbers on the way.

"'It has certainly been a hard day,' said little Hans to himself as he was going to bed, 'but I am glad I did not refuse the Miller, for he is my best friend, and, besides, he is going to give me his wheelbarrow.'

"Early the next morning the Miller came down to get the money for his sack of flour, but little Hans was so tired that he was still in bed.

"'Upon my word,' said the Miller, 'you are very lazy. Really, considering that I am going to give you my wheelbarrow, I think you might work harder. Idleness is a great sin, and I certainly don't like any of my friends to be idle or sluggish. You must not mind my speaking quite plainly to you. Of course, I should not dream of doing so if I were not your friend. But what is the good of friendship if one cannot say exactly what one means? Anybody can say charming things and try to please and to flatter, but a true friend always says unpleasant things, and does not mind giving pain. Indeed, if he is a really true friend he prefers it, for he knows that then he is doing good.'

"'I am very sorry,' said little Hans, rubbing his eyes and pulling off his nightcap. 'But I was so tired that I thought I would lie in bed for a little time, and listen to the birds singing. Do you know that I always work better after hearing the birds sing?'

"'Well, I am glad of that,' said the Miller, clapping little Hans on the back, 'for I want you to come up to the mill as soon as you are dressed, and mend my barn roof for me.'

"Poor little Hans was very anxious to go and work in his garden, for his flowers had not been watered for two days, but he did not like to refuse the Miller, as he was such a good friend to him.

"'Do you think it would be unfriendly of me if I said I was busy?' he inquired in a shy and timid voice.

"'Well, really,' answered the Miller, 'I do not think it is much to ask of you, considering that I am going to give you my wheelbarrow. But, of course, if you refuse, I will go and do it myself.'

"'Oh! On no account,' cried little Hans. And he jumped out of bed, and dressed himself, and went up to the barn.

"He worked there all day long, till sunset, and at sunset the Miller came to see how he was getting on.

"'Have you mended the hole in the roof yet, little Hans?' cried the Miller in a cheery voice.

"'It is quite mended,' answered little Hans, coming down the ladder.

"'Ah!' said the Miller, 'there is no work so delightful as the work one does for others.'

"'It is certainly a great privilege to hear you talk,' answered little Hans, sitting down and wiping his forehead. 'A very great privilege. But I am afraid I shall never have such beautiful ideas as you have.'

"'Oh! They will come to you,' said the Miller. 'But you must take more pains. At present you have only the practice of friendship. Someday you will have the theory also.'

"'Do you really think I shall?' asked little Hans.

"'I have no doubt of it,' answered the Miller, 'but now that you have mended the roof, you had better go home and rest, for I want you to drive my sheep to the mountain tomorrow.'

"Poor little Hans was afraid to say anything to this, and early the next morning the Miller brought his sheep round to the cottage, and Hans started off with them to the mountain. It took him the whole day to get there and back, and when he returned he was so tired that he went off to sleep in his chair, and did not wake up till it was broad daylight.

"'What a delightful time I shall have in my garden,' he said, and he went to work at once.

"But somehow he was never able to look after his flowers at all, for his friend the Miller was always coming round and sending him off on long errands, or getting him to help at the mill. Little Hans was very much distressed at times, as he was afraid his flowers would think he had forgotten them, but he consoled himself by the reflection that the Miller was his best friend. 'Besides,' he used to say, 'he is going to give me his wheel-barrow, and that is an act of pure generosity.'

"So little Hans worked away for the Miller, and the Miller said all kinds of beautiful things about friendship, which Hans took down in a notebook, and used to read over at night, for he was a very good scholar.

"Now it happened that one evening little Hans was sitting by his fireside when a loud rap came at the door. It was a very wild night, and the wind was blowing and roaring round the house so terribly that at first he thought it was merely the storm. But a second rap came, and then a third, louder than either of the others.

"'It is some poor traveler,' said little Hans to himself, and he ran to the door.

"There stood the Miller with a lantern in one hand and a big stick in the other.

"'Dear little Hans,' cried the Miller. 'I am in great trouble.

My little boy has fallen off a ladder and hurt himself, and I am going for the Doctor. But he lives so far away, and it is such a bad night, that it has just occurred to me that it would be much better if you went instead of me. You know I am going to give you my wheelbarrow, and so it is only fair that you should do something for me in return.'

"'Certainly,' cried little Hans. 'I take it quite as a compliment your coming to me, and I will start off at once. But you must lend me your lantern, as the night is so dark that I am afraid I might fall into the ditch.'

"'I am very sorry,' answered the Miller. 'But it is my new lantern, and it would be a great loss to me if anything happened to it.'

"'Well, never mind, I will do without it,' cried little Hans, and he took down his great fur coat, and his warm scarlet cap, and tied a muffler round his throat, and started off.

"What a dreadful storm it was! The night was so black that little Hans could hardly see, and the wind was so strong that he could scarcely stand. However, he was very courageous, and after he had been walking about three hours, he arrived at the Doctor's house, and knocked at the door.

"'Who is there?' cried the Doctor, putting his head out of his bedroom window.

"'Little Hans, Doctor.'

"'What do you want, little Hans?'

"'The Miller's son has fallen from a ladder, and has hurt himself, and the Miller wants you to come at once.'

"'All right!' said the Doctor. And he ordered his horse, and his big boots, and his lantern, and came downstairs, and rode off in the direction of the Miller's house, little Hans trudging behind him.

"But the storm grew worse and worse, and the rain fell in torrents, and little Hans could not see where he was going, or keep up with the horse. At last he lost his way, and wandered off on the moor, which was a very dangerous place, as it was full of deep holes, and there poor little Hans was drowned. His body was found the next day by some goatherds, floating in a great pool of water, and was brought back by them to the cottage.

"Everybody went to little Hans's funeral, as he was so popular, and the Miller was the chief mourner.

"'As I was his best friend,' said the Miller, 'it is only fair that I should have the best place. So he walked at the head of the procession in a long black cloak, and every now and then he wiped his eyes with a big pocket-handkerchief.

"'Little Hans is certainly a great loss to everyone,' said the Blacksmith, when the funeral was over and they were all seated comfortably in the inn, drinking spiced wine and eating sweet cakes.

"'A great loss to me at any rate,' answered the Miller. 'Why, I had as good as given him my wheelbarrow, and now I really don't know what to do with it. It is very much in my way at home, and it is in such bad repair that I could not get anything for it if I sold it. I will certainly take care not to give away anything again. One always suffers for being generous.'"

"Well?" said the Water Rat, after a long pause.

"Well, that is the end," said the Linnet.

"But what became of the Miller?" asked the Water Rat.

"Oh! I really don't know," replied the Linnet. "And I am sure that I don't care."

"It is quite evident then that you have no sympathy in your nature," said the Water Rat.

"I am afraid you don't quite see the moral of the story," remarked the Linnet.

"The what?" screamed the Water Rat.

"The moral."

"Do you mean to say that the story has a moral?"

"Certainly," said the Linnet.

"Well, really," said the Water Rat, in a very angry manner, "I think you should have told me that before you began. If you had done so, I certainly would not have listened to you. In fact, I should have said 'Pooh,' like the critic. However, I can say it now." So he shouted out "Pooh" at the top of his voice, gave a whisk with his tail, and went back into his hole.

"And how do you like the Water Rat?" asked the Duck, who came paddling up some minutes afterward. "He has a great many good points, but for my own part I have a mother's feelings, and I can never look at a confirmed bachelor without the tears coming into my eyes."

"I am rather afraid that I have annoyed him," answered the Linnet. "The fact is that I told him a story with a moral."

"Ah! that is always a very dangerous thing to do," said the Duck.

And I quite agree with her.

The Dog of Montargis

RETOLD BY JAMES BALDWIN

This unusual old story reminds us that loyalty is the virtue that helps us stand fast beside our friends—and our memories of our friends.

I n the old castle of Montargis in France, there was once a stone mantelpiece of workmanship so rare that it was talked about by the whole country. And yet it was not altogether its beauty that caused people to speak of it and remember it. It was famous rather on account of the strange scene that was carved upon it. To those who asked about its meaning, the old custodian of the castle would sometimes tell the following story.

It happened more than five hundred years ago, when this castle was new and strong, and people lived and thought in very different ways than they do now. Among the young men of that time there was none more noble than Aubrey de Montdidier, the nephew of the Count of Montargis; and among all the knights who had favor at the royal court, there was none braver than the young Sieur de Narsac, captain of the king's men at arms.

Now these two men were devoted friends, and whenever their other duties allowed them, they were sure to be in each other's company. Indeed, it was a rare thing to see either of them walking the streets of Paris alone.

"I will meet you at the tournament tomorrow," said Aubrey gaily, one evening, as he was parting from his friend.

"Yes, at the tournament tomorrow," said De Narsac, "and be sure that you come early."

The tournament was to be a grand affair. A gentleman from Provence was to run a tilt with a famous Burgundian knight. Both men were noted for their horsemanship and their skill with the lance. All Paris would be out to see them.

When the time came, De Narsac was at the place appointed. But Aubrey failed to appear. What could it mean? It was not at all like Aubrey to forget his promise; it was seldom that he allowed anything to keep him away from the tournament.

"Have you seen my friend Aubrey today?" De Narsac asked this question a hundred times. Everybody gave the same answer and wondered what had happened.

The day passed and another day came, and still there was no news from Aubrey. De Narsac had called at his friend's lodgings but could learn nothing. The young man had not been seen since the morning before the tournament.

Three days passed, and still not a word. De Narsac was greatly troubled. He knew now that some accident must have happened to Aubrey. But what could it have been?

Early in the morning of the fourth day, he was aroused by a strange noise at his door. He dressed himself in haste and opened it. A dog was crouching there. It was a greyhound, so thin that his ribs stuck out, so weak that he could hardly stand.

De Narsac knew the animal without looking at the collar on his neck. He was Dragon, his friend Aubrey's greyhound—the dog who went with him whenever he went out, the dog who was never seen save in his master's company.

The poor creature tried to stand. His legs trembled from weakness. He swayed from side to side. He wagged his tail feebly and tried to put his nose in De Narsac's hand. De Narsac saw at once that he was half starved.

He led the dog into his room and fed him some warm milk. He bathed the poor fellow's nose and bloodshot eyes with cold water. "Tell me where your master is," he said. Then he set before him a full meal that would have tempted any dog.

The greyhound ate heartily and seemed to be much stronger. He licked De Narsac's hands. Then he ran to the door and tried to make signs to his friend to follow him. He whined pitifully.

De Narsac understood. "You want to lead me to your master, I see." He put on his hat and went out with the dog.

Through the narrow lanes and crooked streets of the old city, Dragon led the way. At each corner he would stop and look back to make sure that De Narsac was following. He went over the long bridge—the only one that spanned the river in those days. Then he trotted out through the gate of St. Martin and into the open country beyond the walls.

In a little while the dog left the main road and took a bypath that led into the forest of Bondy. De Narsac kept his hand on his sword now, for they were on dangerous ground. The forest was a great hangout for robbers and lawless men, and more than one wild and wicked deed had been enacted there.

But Dragon did not go far into the woods. He stopped suddenly near a dense thicket of briers and tangled vines. He whined as though in great distress. Then he took hold of the sleeve of De Narsac's coat, and led him round to the other side of the thicket.

There under a low-spreading oak the grass had been trampled down. There were signs, too, of freshly turned-up earth. With moans of distress the dog stretched himself upon the ground, and with pleading eyes looked up into De Narsac's face.

"Ah, my poor fellow!" said De Narsac, "you have led me here to show me your master's grave." And with that he turned and hurried back to the city, but the dog would not stir from his place.

That afternoon a company of men, led by De Narsac, rode out to the forest. They found in the ground beneath the oak what they had expected—the murdered body of young Aubrey de Montdidier.

"Who could have done this foul deed?" they asked of one another. And then they wept, for they all loved Aubrey.

They made a litter of green branches and laid the body upon it. Then, the dog following them, they carried it back to the city and buried it in the king's cemetery. And all Paris mourned the untimely end of the brave young knight.

After this, the greyhound went to live with the young Sieur de Narsac. He followed the knight wherever he went. He slept in his room and ate from his hand. He seemed to be as much devoted to his new master as he had been to the old.

One morning they went out for a stroll through the city. The streets were crowded, for it was a holiday and all the fine people of Paris were enjoying the sunlight and the fresh air. Dragon, as usual, kept close to the heels of his master.

De Narsac walked down one street and up another, meeting many of his friends, and now and then stopping to talk a little while. Suddenly, as they were passing a corner, the dog leaped forward and planted himself in front of his master. He growled fiercely and crouched as though ready for a spring. His eyes were fixed upon someone in the crowd.

Then, before De Narsac could speak, he leaped forward upon a young man whom he had singled out. The man threw up his arm to protect his throat, but the quickness of the attack and the weight of the dog caused him to fall to the ground. There is no telling what might have followed had not those who were with him beaten the dog with their canes, and driven him away.

De Narsac knew the man. His name was Richard Macaire, and he belonged to the king's bodyguard.

Never before had the greyhound been known to show anger toward any person. "What do you mean by such conduct?" asked his master as they walked homeward. Dragon's only answer was a low growl, but it was the best that he could give. The affair had put a thought into De Narsac's mind which he could not dismiss.

Within less than a week, the thing happened again. This time Macaire was walking in the public garden. De Narsac and the dog were some distance away. But as soon as Dragon saw the man, he rushed at him. It was all that the bystanders could do to keep him from throttling Macaire. De Narsac hurried up and called him away, but the dog's anger was fearful to see.

It was well known in Paris that Macaire and young Aubrey had not been friends. It was remembered that they had had more than one quarrel. And now the people began to talk about the dog's strange actions, and some went so far as to put this and that together.

At last the matter reached the ears of the king. He sent for De Narsac and had a long talk with him. "Come back tomorrow and bring the dog with you," he said. "We must find out more about this strange affair."

The next day De Narsac, with Dragon at his heels, was admitted into the king's audience room. The king was seated in his great chair, and many knights and men at arms were standing around him. Hardly had De Narsac stepped inside when the dog leaped quickly forward. He had seen Macaire, and had singled him out from among all the rest. He sprang upon him. He would have torn him in pieces if no one had interfered.

There was now only one way to explain the matter.

"This greyhound," said De Narsac, "is here to denounce the Chevalier Macaire as the slayer of his master, young Aubrey de Montdidier. He demands that justice be done, and that the murderer be punished for his crime."

The Chevalier Macaire was pale and trembling. He stammered a denial of his guilt, and declared that the dog was a dangerous beast, and ought to be put out of the way. "Shall a soldier in the service of the king be accused by a dog?" he cried. "Shall he be condemned on such testimony as this? I, too, demand justice."

"Let the judgment of God decide!" cried the knights who were present.

And so the king declared that there should be a trial by the judgment of God. For in those rude times it was a very common thing to determine guilt or innocence in this way—that is, by a combat between the accuser and the accused. In such cases it was believed that God would always aid the cause of the innocent and bring about the defeat of the guilty.

The combat was to take place that very afternoon in the great common by the riverside. The king's herald made a public announcement of it, naming the dog as the accuser and the Chevalier Macaire as the accused. A great crowd of people assembled to see this strange trial by the judgment of God.

The king and his officers were there to make sure that no injustice was done to either the man or the dog. The man was allowed to defend himself with a short stick. The dog was given a barrel into which he might run if too closely pressed.

At a signal the combat began. Macaire stood on his guard while the dog darted swiftly around him, dodging the blows that were aimed at him, and trying to get at his enemy's throat. The man seemed to have lost all his courage. His breath came short and quick. He was trembling from head to foot.

Suddenly the dog leaped upon him and threw him to the ground. In great terror Macaire cried to the king for mercy and acknowledged his guilt.

"It is the judgment of God!" cried the king.

The officers rushed in and dragged the dog away before he could harm the guilty man. Macaire was hurried off to the punishment which his crimes deserved.

And this is the scene that was carved on the old mantelpiece in the castle of Montargis—this strange trial by the judgment of God. Is it not fitting that a dog so faithful, devoted, and brave should have his memory thus preserved in stone?

Emerson on Friendship

Emerson writes that friendships are gifts and expressions of God; they form when the divine spirit in one individual finds the divine spirit in another, and "both deride and cancel the thick walls of individual character, relation, age, sex, and circumstance." The essay "Friendship" was first published in 1841.

I do not wish to treat friendships daintily, but with roughest courage. When they are real, they are not glass threads or frost-work, but the solidest thing we know. For now, after so many ages of experience, what do we know of nature, or of ourselves? Not one step has man taken toward the solution of the problem of his destiny. In one condemnation of folly stand the whole universe of men. But the sweet sincerity of joy and peace, which I draw from this alliance with my brother's soul, is the nut itself whereof all nature and all thought is but the husk and shell.

Happy is the house that shelters a friend! It might well be built, like a festal bower or arch, to entertain him a single day. Happier, if he know the solemnity of that relation, and honor its law! He who offers himself a candidate for that covenant comes up like an Olympian to the great games where the firstborn of the world are the competitors. He proposes himself for contests where Time, Want, Danger are in the lists, and he alone is victor who has truth enough in his constitution to preserve the delicacy of his beauty from the wear and tear of all these. The gifts of fortune may be present or absent, but all the hap in that contest depends on intrinsic nobleness and the contempt of trifles. . . .

A friend is a person with whom I may be sincere. Before him, I may think aloud. I am arrived at last in the presence of a man so real and equal that I may drop even those undermost garments of dissimulation, courtesy, and second thought, which men never put off, and may deal with him with the simplicity and wholeness with which one chemical atom meets another. Sincerity is the luxury allowed, like diadems and authority, only to the highest rank, that being permitted to speak truth as having none above it to court or conform unto.

Every man alone is sincere. At the entrance of a second person hypocrisy begins. We parry and fend the approach of our fellow man by compliments, by gossip, by amusements, by affairs. We cover up our thought from him under a hundred folds. I knew a man who, under a certain religious frenzy, cast off this drapery, and, omitting all compliments and commonplace, spoke to the conscience of every person he encountered, and that with great insight and beauty. At first he was resisted, and all men agreed he was mad. By persisting, as indeed he could not help doing, for some time in this course, he attained to the advantage of bringing every man of his acquaintance into true relations with him. No man would think of speaking falsely with him, or of putting him off with any chat of markets or reading rooms. But every man was constrained by so much sincerity to the like plain dealing, and what love of nature, what poetry, what symbol of truth he had, he did certainly show him.

But to most of us society shows not its face and eye, but its side and its back. To stand in true relations with men in a false age is worth a fit of insanity, is it not? We can seldom go erect. Almost every man we meet requires some civility, requires to be humored; he has some fame, some talent, some whim of religion or philanthropy in his head that is not to be questioned, and which spoils all conversation with him.

But a friend is a sane man who exercises not my ingenuity, but me. My friend gives me entertainment without requiring any stipulation on my part. A friend, therefore, is a sort of paradox in nature. I who alone am, I who see nothing in nature whose existence I can affirm with equal evidence to my own, behold now the semblance of my being in all its height, variety, and curiosity reiterated in a foreign form; so that a friend may well be reckoned the masterpiece of nature.

The Enchanted Bluff

WILLA CATHER

This is a story about the kind of commonplace dreams and adventures friends share in youth. Memories of such times spent together make friendships span the years and miles that later separate us.

We had our swim before sundown, and while we were cooking our supper the oblique rays of light made a dazzling glare on the white sand about us. The translucent red ball itself sank behind the brown stretches of corn field as we sat down to eat, and the warm layer of air that had rested over the water and our clean sand bar grew fresher and smelled of the rank ironweed and sunflowers growing on the flatter shore. The river was brown and sluggish, like any other of the half-dozen streams that water the Nebraska corn lands. On one shore was an irregular line of bald clay bluffs where a few scrub oaks with thick trunks and flat, twisted tops threw light shadows on the long grass. The western shore was low and level, with corn fields that stretched to the skyline, and all along the water's edge were little sandy coves and beaches where slim cottonwoods and willow saplings flickered.

The turbulence of the river in springtime discouraged milling, and, beyond keeping the old red bridge in repair, the busy farmers did not concern themselves with the stream; so the Sandtown boys were left in undisputed possession. In the autumn we hunted quail through the miles of stubble and fodder land along the flat shore, and, after the winter skating season was over and the ice had gone out, the spring freshets and flooded bottoms gave us our great excitement of the year. The channel was never the same for two successive seasons. Every spring the swollen stream undermined a bluff to the east, or bit out a few acres of corn field to the west and whirled the soil away to deposit it in spumy mud banks somewhere else. When the water fell low in midsummer, new sand bars were thus exposed to dry and whiten in the August sun. Sometimes these were banked so firmly that the fury of the next freshet failed to unseat them; the little willow seedlings emerged triumphantly from the yellow froth, broke into spring leaf, shot up into summer growth, and with their mesh of roots bound together the moist sand beneath them against the batterings of another April. Here and there a cottonwood soon glittered among them, quivering in the low current of air that, even on breathless days when the dust hung like smoke above the wagon road, trembled along the face of the water.

It was on such an island, in the third summer of its yellow green, that we built our watch fire; not in the thicket of dancing willow wands, but on the level terrace of fine sand which had been added that spring; a little new bit of world, beautifully ridged with ripple marks, and strewn with the tiny skeletons of turtles and fish, all as white and dry as if they had been expertly cured. We had been careful not to mar the freshness of the place, although we often swam to it on summer evenings and lay on the sand to rest.

This was our last watch fire of the year, and there were reasons why I should remember it better than any of the others. Next week the other boys were to file back to their old places in the Sandtown High School, but I was to go up to the Divide to teach my first country school in the Norwegian district. I was already homesick at the thought of quitting the boys with whom I had always played; of leaving the river, and going up into a windy plain that was all windmills and corn fields and big pastures; where there was nothing willful or unmanageable in the landscape, no new islands, and no chance of unfamiliar birds—such as often followed the watercourses.

Other boys came and went and used the river for fishing or skating, but we six were sworn to the spirit of the stream, and we were friends mainly because of the river. There were the two Hassler boys, Fritz and Otto, sons of the little German tailor. They were the youngest of us; ragged boys of ten and twelve, with sunburned hair, weather-stained faces, and pale blue eyes. Otto, the elder, was the best mathematician in school, and clever at his books, but he always dropped out in the spring term as if the river could not get on without him. He and Fritz caught the fat, horned catfish and sold them about the town, and they lived so much in the water that they were as brown and sandy as the river itself.

There was Percy Pound, a fat, freckled boy with chubby cheeks, who took half a dozen boys' story-papers and was always being kept in for reading detective stories behind his desk. There was Tip Smith, destined by his freckles and red hair to be the buffoon in all our games, though he walked like a timid little old man and had a funny, cracked laugh. Tip worked hard in his father's grocery store every afternoon and swept it out before school in the morning. Even his recreations were laborious. He collected cigarette cards and tin tobacco-tags indefatigably, and would sit for hours humped up over a snarling little scroll-saw which he kept in his attic. His dearest possessions were some little pill bottles that purported to contain grains of wheat from the Holy Land, water from the Jordan and the Dead Sea, and earth from the Mount of Olives. His father had bought these dull things from a Baptist missionary who peddled them, and Tip seemed to derive great satisfaction from their remote origin.

The tall boy was Arthur Adams. He had fine hazel eyes that were almost too reflective and sympathetic for a boy, and such a pleasant voice that we all loved to hear him read aloud. Even when he had to read poetry aloud at school, no one ever thought of laughing. To be sure, he was not at school very much of the time. He was seventeen and should have finished the High School the year before, but he was always off somewhere with his gun. Arthur's mother was dead, and his father, who was feverishly absorbed in promoting schemes, wanted to send the boy away to school and get him off his hands; but Arthur always begged off for another year and promised to study. I remember him as a tall, brown boy with an intelligent face, always lounging among a lot of us little fellows, laughing at us oftener than with us, but such a soft, satisfied laugh that we felt rather flattered when we provoked it. In after-years people said that Arthur had been given to evil ways even as a lad, and it is true that we often saw him with the gambler's sons and with old Spanish Fanny's boy, but if he learned anything ugly in their company he never betrayed it to us. We would have followed Arthur anywhere, and I am bound to say that he led us into no worse places than the cattail marshes and the stubble fields. These, then, were the boys who camped with me that summer night upon the sand bar.

After we finished our supper we beat the willow thicket for driftwood. By the time we had collected enough, night had fallen, and the pungent, weedy smell from the shore increased with the coolness. We threw ourselves down about the fire and made another futile effort to show Percy Pound the Little Dipper. We had tried it often before, but he could never be got past the big one.

"You see those three big stars just below the handle, with the bright one in the middle?" said Otto Hassler. "That's Orion's belt, and the bright one is the clasp." I crawled behind Otto's shoulder and sighted up his arm to the star that seemed perched upon the tip of his steady forefinger. The Hassler boys did seine-fishing at night, and they knew a good many stars.

Percy gave up the Little Dipper and lay back on the sand, his hands clasped under his head. "I can see the North Star," he announced, contentedly, pointing toward it with his big toe. "Anyone might get lost and need to know that."

We all looked up at it.

"How do you suppose Columbus felt when his compass didn't point north anymore?" Tip asked.

Otto shook his head. "My father says that there was another North Star once, and that maybe this one won't last always. I wonder what would happen to us down here if anything went wrong with it?"

Arthur chuckled. "I wouldn't worry, Ott. Nothing's apt to happen to it in your time. Look at the Milky Way! There must be lots of good dead Indians."

We lay back and looked, meditating, at the dark cover of the world. The gurgle of the water had become heavier. We had often noticed a mutinous, complaining note in it at night, quite different from its cheerful daytime chuckle, and seeming like the voice of a much deeper and more powerful stream. Our water had always these two moods: the one of sunny complaisance, the other of inconsolable, passionate regret.

"Queer how the stars are all in sort of diagrams," remarked Otto. "You could do most any proposition in geometry with 'em. They always look as if they meant something. Some folks say everybody's fortune is all written out in the stars, don't they?"

"They believe so in the old country," Fritz affirmed.

But Arthur only laughed at him. "You're thinking of Napoleon, Fritzey. He had a star that went out when he began to lose battles. I guess the stars don't keep any close tally on Sandtown folks."

We were speculating on how many times we could count a hundred before the evening star went down behind the corn fields, when someone cried, "There comes the moon, and it's as big as a cart wheel!"

We all jumped up to greet it as it swam over the bluffs behind us. It came up like a galleon in full sail; an enormous, barbaric thing, red as an angry heathen god.

"When the moon came up red like that, the Aztecs used to sacrifice their prisoners on the temple top," Percy announced.

"Go on, Perce. You got that out of *Golden Days*. Do you believe that, Arthur?" I appealed.

Arthur answered, quite seriously: "Like as not. The moon was one of their gods. When my father was in Mexico City, he saw the stone where they used to sacrifice their prisoners."

As we dropped down by the fire again someone asked whether the Mound-Builders were older than the Aztecs. When we once got upon the Mound-Builders, we never willingly got away from them, and we were still conjecturing when we heard a loud splash in the water.

"Must have been a big cat jumping," said Fritz. "They do sometimes. They must see bugs in the dark. Look what a track the moon makes!"

There was a long, silvery streak on the water, and where the current fretted over a big log, it boiled up like gold pieces.

"Suppose there ever *was* any gold hid away in this old river?" Fritz asked. He lay like a little brown Indian, close to the fire, his chin on his hand and his bare feet in the air. His brother laughed at him, but Arthur took his suggestion seriously.

"Some of the Spaniards thought there was gold up here somewhere. Seven cities chuck full of gold, they had it, and Coronado and his men came up to hunt it. The Spaniards were all over this country once."

Percy looked interested. "Was that before the Mormons went through?"

We all laughed at this.

"Long enough before. Before the Pilgrim Fathers, Perce. Maybe they came along this very river. They always followed the watercourses."

"I wonder where this river really does begin?" Tip mused. That was an old and a favorite mystery which the map did not clearly explain. On the map the little black line stopped somewhere in western Kansas; but since rivers generally rose in mountains, it was only reasonable to suppose that ours came from the Rockies. Its destination, we knew, was the Missouri, and the Hassler boys always maintained that we could embark at Sandtown in floodtime, follow our noses, and eventually arrive at New Orleans. Now they took up their old argument. "If us boys had grit enough to try it, it wouldn't take no time to get to Kansas City and St. Joe."

We began to talk about the places we wanted to go to. The Hassler boys wanted to see the stockyards in Kansas City, and Percy wanted to see a big store in Chicago. Arthur was interlocutor and did not betray himself.

"Now it's your turn, Tip."

Tip rolled over on his elbow and poked the fire, and his eyes looked shyly out of his queer, tight little face. "My place is awful far away. My Uncle Bill told me about it."

Tip's Uncle Bill was a wanderer, bitten with mining fever, who had drifted into Sandtown with a broken arm, and when it was well had drifted out again.

"Where is it?"

"Aw, it's down in New Mexico somewheres. There aren't no railroads or anything. You have to go on mules, and you run out of water before you get there and have to drink canned tomatoes."

"Well, go on, kid. What's it like when you do get there?"

Tip sat up and excitedly began his story.

"There's a big red rock there that goes right up out of the sand for about nine hundred feet. The country's flat all around it, and this here rock goes up all by itself, like a monument. They call it the Enchanted Bluff down there, because no white man has ever been on top of it. The sides are smooth rock, and straight up, like a wall. The Indians say that hundreds of years ago, before the Spaniards came, there was a village away up there in the air. The tribe that lived there had some sort of steps, made out of wood and bark, hung down over the face of the bluff, and the braves went down to hunt and carried water up in big jars swung on their backs. They kept a big supply of water and dried meat up there, and never went down except to hunt. They were a peaceful tribe that made cloth and pottery, and they went up there to get out of the wars. You see, they could pick off any war party that tried to get up their steps. The Indians say they were a handsome people, and they had some sort of queer religion. Uncle Bill thinks they were Cliff-Dwellers who had got into trouble and left home. They weren't fighters, anyhow.

"One time the braves were down hunting and an awful storm came up—a kind of waterspout—and when they got back to their rock they found their little staircase had been all broken to pieces, and only a few steps were left hanging away up in the air.

While they were camped at the foot of the rock, wondering what to do, a war party from the north came along and massacred 'em to a man, with all the old folks and women looking on from the rock. Then the war party went on south and left the village to get down the best way they could. Of course they never got down. They starved to death up there, and when the war party came back on their way north, they could hear the children crying from the edge of the bluff where they had crawled out, but they didn't see a sign of a grown Indian, and nobody has ever been up there since."

We exclaimed at this dolorous legend and sat up.

"There couldn't have been many people up there," Percy demurred. "How big is the top, Tip?"

"Oh, pretty big. Big enough so that the rock doesn't look nearly as tall as it is. The top's bigger than the base. The bluff is sort of worn away for several hundred feet up. That's one reason it's so hard to climb.'"

I asked how the Indians got up, in the first place.

"Nobody knows how they got up or when. A hunting party came along once and saw that there was a town up there, and that was all."

Otto rubbed his chin and looked thoughtful. "Of course there must be some way to get up there. Couldn't people get a rope over someway and pull a ladder up?"

Tip's little eyes were shining with excitement. "I know a way. Me and Uncle Bill talked it all over. There's a kind of rocket that would take a rope over—life-savers use 'em—and then you could hoist a rope ladder and peg it down at the bottom and make it tight with guy ropes on the other side. I'm going to climb that there bluff, and I've got it all planned out."

Fritz asked what he expected to find when he got up there.

"Bones, maybe, or the ruins of their town, or pottery, or some of their idols. There might be 'most anything up there. Anyhow, I want to see."

"Sure nobody else has been up there, Tip?" Arthur asked.

"Dead sure. Hardly anybody ever goes down there. Some hunters tried to cut steps in the rock once, but they didn't get higher than a man can reach. The Bluff's all red granite, and Uncle Bill thinks it's a boulder the glaciers left. It's a queer place, anyhow. Nothing but cactus and desert for hundreds of miles, and yet right under the Bluff there's good water and plenty of grass. That's why the bison used to go down there."

Suddenly we heard a scream above our fire, and jumped up to see a dark, slim bird floating southward far above us—a whooping crane, we knew by her cry and her long neck. We ran to the edge of the island, hoping we might see her alight, but she wavered southward along the river course until we lost her. The Hassler boys declared that by the look of the heavens it must be after midnight, so we threw more wood on our fire, put on our jackets, and curled down in the warm sand. Several of us pretended to doze, but I fancy we were really thinking about Tip's Bluff and the extinct people. Over in the wood the ring doves were calling mournfully to one another, and once we heard a dog bark, far away. "Somebody getting into old Tommy's melon patch," Fritz murmured sleepily, but nobody answered him. By and by Percy spoke out of the shadows.

"Say, Tip, when you go down there will you take me with you?"

"Maybe."

"Suppose one of us beats you down there, Tip?"

"Whoever gets to the Bluff first has got to promise to tell the rest of us exactly what he finds," remarked one of the Hassler boys, and to this we all readily assented.

Somewhat reassured, I dropped off to sleep. I must have dreamed about a race for the Bluff, for I awoke in a kind of fear that other people were getting ahead of me and that I was losing my chance. I sat up in my damp clothes and looked at the other boys, who lay tumbled in uneasy attitudes about the dead fire. It was still dark, but the sky was blue with the last wonderful azure of night. The stars glistened like crystal globes, and trembled as if they shone through a depth of clear water. Even as I watched, they began to pale and the sky brightened. Day came suddenly, almost instantaneously. I turned for another look at the blue night, and it was gone. Everywhere the birds began to call, and all manner of little insects began to chirp and hop about in the willows. A breeze sprang up from the west and brought the heavy smell of ripened corn. The boys rolled over and shook themselves. We stripped and plunged into the river just as the sun came up over the windy bluffs.

When I came home to Sandtown at Christmastime, we skated out to our island and talked over the whole project of the Enchanted Bluff, renewing our resolution to find it.

Although that was twenty years ago, none of us have ever climbed the Enchanted Bluff. Percy Pound is a stockbroker in

Kansas City and will go nowhere that his red touring car cannot carry him. Otto Hassler went on the railroad and lost his foot braking; after which he and Fritz succeeded their father as the town tailors.

Arthur sat about the sleepy little town all his life—he died before he was twenty-five. The last time I saw him, when I was home on one of my college vacations, he was sitting in a steamer chair under a cottonwood tree in the little yard behind one of the two Sandtown saloons. He was very untidy and his hand was not steady, but when he rose, unabashed, to greet me, his eyes were as clear and warm as ever. When I had talked with him for an hour and heard him laugh again, I wondered how it was that when Nature had taken such pains with a man, from his hands to the arch of his long foot, she had ever lost him in Sandtown. He joked about Tip Smith's Bluff, and declared he was going down there just as soon as the weather got cooler; he thought the Grand Canyon might be worthwhile, too.

I was perfectly sure when I left him that he would never get beyond the high plank fence and the comfortable shade of the cottonwood. And, indeed, it was under that very tree that he died one summer morning.

Tip Smith still talks about going to New Mexico. He married a slatternly, unthrifty country girl, has been much tied to a perambulator, and has grown stooped and gray from irregular meals and broken sleep. But the worst of his difficulties are now over, and he has, as he says, come into easy water. When I was last in Sandtown I walked home with him late one moonlit night, after he had balanced his cash and shut up his store. We took the long way around and sat down on the schoolhouse steps, and between us we quite revived the romance of the lone red rock and the extinct people. Tip insists that he still means to go down there, but he thinks now he will wait until his boy Bert is old enough to go with him. Bert has been let into the story, and thinks of nothing but the Enchanted Bluff.

Friendship Sweetening to the Evening of Life

THOMAS JEFFERSON

Friendship is one virtue that may grow more dear to us in the twilight of life. This letter from Thomas Jefferson to John Adams gives us a glimpse into one of the most remarkable friendships in our nation's political history. These men were longtime political adversaries, but they were also wise enough and great-hearted enough to know that honest philosophical differences do not have to scar personal friendships. When he learned of schemes to "draw a curtain of separation" between the two of them, Jefferson wrote this eloquent letter to his old comrade.

Less than three years later, lying on his deathbed, John Adams reassured himself with the words, "Thomas Jefferson survives!" He did not know that five hundred miles away at Monticello, Jefferson was dying as well. On July 4, 1826, exactly fifty years after the birth of the nation they had helped create, two great friends and patriots departed this earth together.

To John Adams
Monticello, October 12, 1823

Dear Sir,

I do not write with the ease which your letter of September
the 18th supposes. Crippled wrists and fingers make writing
slow and laborious. But while writing to you, I lose the sense of
these things in the recollection of ancient times, when youth
and health made happiness out of everything. I forget for a
while the hoary winter of age, when we can think of nothing
but how to keep ourselves warm, and how to get rid of our
heavy hours until the friendly hand of death shall rid us of all
at once. Against this *tedium vitae,* however, I am fortunately
mounted on a hobby, which, indeed, I should have better man-
aged some thirty or forty years ago; but whose easy amble is still
sufficient to give exercise and amusement to an octogenary
rider. This is the establishment of a University, on a scale more
comprehensive and in a country more healthy and central than
our old William and Mary, which these obstacles have long kept
in a state of languor and inefficiency. But the tardiness with
which such works proceed may render it doubtful whether I
shall live to see it go into action.

Putting aside these things, however, for the present I write
this letter as due to a friendship coeval with our government,
and now attempted to be poisoned, when too late in life to be
replaced by new affections. I had for some time observed in the
public papers dark hints and mysterious innuendoes of a corre-
spondence of yours with a friend, to whom you had opened your

bosom without reserve, and which was to be made public by that friend or his representative. And now it is said to be actually published. It has not yet reached us, but extracts have been given, and such as seemed most likely to draw a curtain of separation between you and myself. Were there no other motive than that of indignation against the author of this outrage on private confidence, whose shaft seems to have been aimed at yourself more particularly, this would make it the duty of every honorable mind to disappoint that aim, by opposing to its impression a sevenfold shield of apathy and insensibility. With me, however, no such armor is needed. The circumstances of the times in which we have happened to live, and the partiality of our friends at a particular period, placed us in a state of apparent opposition, which some might suppose to be personal also; and there might not be wanting those who wished to make it so, by filling our ears with malignant falsehoods, by dressing up hideous phantoms of their own creation, presenting them to you under my name, to me under yours, and endeavouring to instill into our minds things concerning each other the most destitute of truth. And if there had been, at any time, a moment when we were off our guard, and in a temper to let the whispers of these people make us forget what we had known of each other for so many years, and years of so much trial, yet all men who have attended to the workings of the human mind, who have seen the false colors under which passion sometimes dresses the actions and motives of others, have seen also those passions subsiding with time and reflection, dissipating like mists before the rising sun, and restoring to us the sight of all things in their true shape and colors. It would be strange indeed if, at our years, we were to go back an age to hunt up imaginary or forgotten facts, to disturb the repose of affections so sweetening to the evening of our lives. Be assured, my dear Sir, that I am incapable of receiving the slightest impression from the effort now made to plant thorns on the pillow of age, worth and wisdom, and to sow tares between friends who have been such for near half a century. Beseeching you then, not to suffer your mind to be disquieted by this wicked attempt to poison its peace, and praying you to throw it by among the things which have never happened, I add sincere assurances of my unabated and constant attachment, friendship, and respect.

The Great Commandment

MATTHEW 22:37–40

Thou shalt love the Lord thy God with all thy heart,
    and with all thy soul, and with all thy mind.
This is the first and great commandment.
    And the second is like unto it;
Thou shalt love thy neighbour as thyself.
On these two commandments hang all the law
    and the prophets.

Helen Keller and Anne Sullivan

HELEN KELLER

There is no friendship more sacred than that between student and teacher, and one of the greatest of these was the friendship of Helen Keller (1880–1968) and Anne Mansfield Sullivan (1866–1936).

Illness destroyed Helen Keller's sight and hearing when she was not yet two years old, leaving her cut off from the world. For nearly five years she grew up, as she later described it, "wild and unruly, giggling and chuckling to express pleasure; kicking, scratching, uttering the choked screams of the deaf-mute to indicate the opposite."

Anne Sullivan's arrival at the Kellers' Alabama home from the Perkins Institution for the Blind in Boston changed Helen's life. Sullivan herself had been half-blind from an eye infection from which she never fully recovered, and she came to Helen with experience, unbending dedication, and love. Through the sense of touch she was able to make contact with the young girl's mind, and within three years she had taught Helen to read and write in braille. By sixteen, Helen could speak well enough to go to preparatory school and college. She graduated cum laude from Radcliffe in 1904, and devoted the rest of her life to helping the

blind and deaf-blind, as her teacher had done. The two women contin-
ued their remarkable friendship until Anne's death.

Helen wrote about Anne Mansfield's arrival in her autobiography,
The Story of My Life.

The most important day I remember in all my life is the one on which my teacher, Anne Mansfield Sullivan, came to me. I am filled with wonder when I consider the immeasurable contrasts between the two lives which it connects. It was the third of March, 1887, three months before I was seven years old.

On the afternoon of that eventful day, I stood on the porch, dumb, expectant. I guessed vaguely from my mother's signs and from the hurrying to and fro in the house that something unusual was about to happen, so I went to the door and waited on the steps. The afternoon sun penetrated the mass of honeysuckle that covered the porch, and fell on my upturned face. My fingers lingered almost unconsciously on the familiar leaves and blossoms which had just come forth to greet the sweet Southern spring. I did not know what the future held of marvel or surprise for me. Anger and bitterness had preyed upon me continually for weeks and a deep languor had succeeded this passionate struggle.

Have you ever been at sea in a dense fog, when it seemed as if a tangible white darkness shut you in, and the great ship, tense and anxious, groped her way toward the shore with plummet and sounding-line, and you waited with beating heart for something to happen? I was like that ship before my education began, only I was without compass or sounding-line, and had no way of knowing how near the harbor was. "Light! Give me light!" was the wordless cry of my soul, and the light of love shone on me in that very hour.

I felt approaching footsteps. I stretched out my hand as I supposed to my mother. Someone took it, and I was caught up and held close in the arms of her who had come to reveal all things to me, and, more than all things else, to love me.

The morning after my teacher came she led me into her room and gave me a doll. The little blind children at the Perkins Institution had sent it and Laura Bridgman had dressed it; but I did not know this until afterward. When I had played with it a little while, Miss Sullivan slowly spelled into my hand the word "d-o-l-l." I was at once interested in this finger play and tried to imitate it. When I finally succeeded in making the letters correctly I was flushed with childish pleasure and pride. Running downstairs to my mother I held up my hand and made the letters for doll. I did not know that I was spelling a word or even that words existed; I was simply making my fingers go in monkeylike imitation. In the days that followed I learned to spell in this uncomprehending way a great many words, among them *pin, hat, cup,* and a few verbs like *sit, stand,* and *walk.* But my teacher had been with me several weeks before I understood that everything has a name.

One day, while I was playing with my new doll, Miss Sullivan put my big rag doll into my lap also, spelled "d-o-l-l," and tried to make me understand that "d-o-l-l" applied to both. Earlier in the day we had had a tussle over the words "m-u-g" and "w-a-t-e-r." Miss Sullivan had tried to impress it upon me that "m-u-g" is *mug* and that "w-a-t-e-r" is *water*, but I persisted in confounding the two. In despair she had dropped the subject for the time, only to renew it at the first opportunity. I became impatient at her repeated attempts and, seizing the new doll, I dashed it upon the floor. I was keenly delighted when I felt the fragments of the broken doll at my feet. Neither sorrow nor regret followed my passionate outburst. I had not loved the doll. In the still, dark world in which I lived there was no strong sentiment or tenderness. I felt my teacher sweep the fragments to one side of the hearth, and I had a sense of satisfaction that the cause of my discomfort was removed. She brought me my hat, and I knew I was going out into the warm sunshine. This thought, if a wordless sensation may be called a thought, made me hop and skip with pleasure.

We walked down the path to the well-house, attracted by the fragrance of the honeysuckle with which it was covered. Someone was drawing water and my teacher placed my hand under the spout. As the cool stream gushed over one hand she spelled into the other the word water, first slowly, then rapidly. I stood still, my whole attention fixed upon the motions of her fingers. Suddenly I felt a misty consciousness as of something forgotten—a thrill of returning thought; and somehow the mystery of language was revealed to me. I knew then that "w-a-t-e-r" meant the wonderful cool something that was flowing over my hand. That living word awakened my soul, gave it light, hope, joy, set it free! There were barriers still, it is true, but barriers that could in time be swept away.

I left the well-house eager to learn. Everything had a name, and each name gave birth to a new thought. As we returned to the house every object which I touched seemed to quiver with life. That was because I saw everything with the strange, new sight that had come to me. On entering the door I remembered the doll I had broken. I felt my way to the hearth and picked up the pieces. I tried vainly to put them together. Then my eyes filled with tears; for I realized what I had done, and for the first time I felt repentance and sorrow.

I learned a great many new words that day. I do not remember what they all were; but I do know that *mother, father, sister, teacher* were among them—words that were to make the world blossom for me, "like Aaron's rod, with flowers." It would have been difficult to find a happier child than I was as I lay in my crib at the close of that eventful day and lived over the joys it had brought me, and for the first time longed for a new day to come.

Anne Mansfield, in her letters, described the "miracle" she saw taking place in Helen.

March 20, 1887

My heart is singing for joy this morning. A miracle has happened! The light of understanding has shone upon my little pupil's mind, and behold, all things are changed!

The wild little creature of two weeks ago has been transformed into a gentle child. She is sitting by me as I write, her face serene and happy, crocheting a long red chain of Scotch wool. She learned the stitch this week, and is very proud of the achievement. When she succeeded in making a chain that would reach across the room, she patted herself on the arm and put the first work of her hands lovingly against her cheek. She lets me kiss her now, and when she is in a particularly gentle mood, she will sit in my lap for a minute or two; but she does not return my caresses. The great step—the step that counts—has been taken. The little savage has learned her first lesson in obedience, and finds the yoke easy. It now remains my pleasant task to direct and mold the beautiful intelligence that is beginning to stir in the child-soul. Already people remark at the change in Helen. Her father looks in at us morning and evening as he goes to and from his office, and sees her contentedly stringing her beads or making horizontal lines on her sewing card, and exclaims, "How quiet she is!" When I came, her movements were so insistent that one always felt there was something unnatural and almost weird about her. I have noticed also that she eats much less, a fact which troubles her father so much that he is anxious to get her home. He says she is homesick. I don't agree with him; but I suppose we shall have to leave our little bower very soon.

Helen has learned several nouns this week. "M-u-g" and "m-i-l-k," have given her more trouble than other words. When she spells "milk," she points to the mug, and when she spells "mug," she makes the sign for pouring or drinking, which shows that she has confused the words. She has no idea yet that everything has a name.

April 5, 1887

I must write you a line this morning because something very important has happened. Helen has taken the second great step in her education. She has learned that *everything has a name, and that the manual alphabet is the key to everything she wants to know.*

In a previous letter I think I wrote you that "mug" and "milk" had given Helen more trouble than all the rest. She confused the nouns with the verb "drink." She didn't know the word for "drink," but went through the pantomime of drinking whenever she spelled "mug" or "milk." This morning, while she was washing, she wanted to know the name for "water." When she wants to know the name of anything, she points to it and pats my hand. I spelled "w-a-t-e-r" and thought no more about it until after breakfast. Then it occurred to me that with the help of this new word I might succeed in straightening out the "mug-milk" difficulty. We went out to the pump-house, and I made Helen hold her mug under the spout while I pumped. As the cold water gushed forth, filling the mug, I spelled "w-a-t-e-r" in Helen's free hand. The word coming so close upon the sensation of cold water rushing over her hand seemed to startle her. She dropped the mug and stood as one transfixed. A new light came into her face. She spelled "water" several times. Then she dropped on the ground and asked for its name and pointed to the pump and the trellis, and suddenly turning round she asked for my name. I spelled "Teacher." Just then the nurse brought Helen's little sister into the pump-house, and Helen spelled "baby" and pointed to the nurse. All the way back to the house she was highly excited, and learned the name of every object she touched, so that in a few hours she had added thirty new words to her vocabulary. Here are some of them: *Door, open, shut, give, go, come,* and a great many more.

P.S.—I didn't finish my letter in time to get it posted last night; so I shall add a line. Helen got up this morning like a radiant fairy. She has flitted from object to object, asking the name of everything and kissing me for very gladness. Last night when I got in bed, she stole into my arms of her own accord and kissed me for the first time, and I thought my heart would burst, so full was it of joy.

The House by the Side of the Road

SAM WALTER FOSS

New England poet Sam Walter Foss (1858–1911) evokes the age-old image of a humble house where the weary traveler finds a welcome—a house such as Baucis and Philemon's—to remind us that we are here to help one another along life's journey. Friends are "help-mates" to each other.

There are hermit souls that live withdrawn
    In the peace of their self-content;
There are souls, like stars, that swell apart,
    In a fellowless firmament;
There are pioneer souls that blaze their paths
    Where highways never ran;
But let me live by the side of the road
    And be a friend to man.

Let me live in a house by the side of the road,
    Where the race of men go by—
The men who are good and the men who are bad,
    As good and as bad as I.
I would not sit in the scorner's seat,
    Or hurl the cynic's ban;
Let me live in a house by the side of the road
    And be a friend to man.

I see from my house by the side of the road,
    By the side of the highway of life,
The men who press with the ardor of hope,
    The men who are faint with the strife.
But I turn not away from their smiles nor their tears—
    Both parts of an infinite plan;
Let me live in my house by the side of the road
    And be a friend to man.

Let me live in my house by the side of the road
    Where the race of men go by—
They are good, they are bad, they are weak, they are strong.
    Wise, foolish—so am I.
Then why should I sit in the scorner's seat
    Or hurl the cynic's ban?—
Let me live in my house by the side of the road
    And be a friend to man.

How Robin Hood Met Little John

ADAPTED FROM HENRY GILBERT

Every once in a while, it takes a legendary outlaw to teach lessons about fairness, generosity, chivalry, and comradeship. Robin Hood and his band of merry men ranged the forests of Sherwood, in Nottinghamshire, and Barnsdale, in Yorkshire, during the days when King Richard the Lionhearted was far away fighting in the Crusades, and the cunning, greedy Prince John ruled in his absence. In this story, good sportsmanship—grace in victory, humor in defeat—makes good friendship.

Once Robin Hood was journeying through the forest of Barnsdale when he came to a broad stream crossed by a narrow beam of oak. It was wide enough for only one man to cross at a time, and, of course, had no railing. Robin walked some two or three feet along it, when on the other bank a tall man appeared and, jumping onto the bridge, also began to cross it.

They stopped and frowned at each other when they were but some ten feet apart.

"Where are your manners, fellow?" Robin called. "Couldn't you see I was already on the bridge before you placed your great big feet on it? Go back!"

"Go back yourself, acornhead," retorted the other. "The small jack should always give way to the big pot."

"You're a stranger in these parts, you chucklehead," said Robin. "Your currish tongue betrays you. But I'll give you a good Barnsdale lesson, if you don't retreat and let me pass." Saying which, he took up his bow and drew an arrow. The tall man, with a half-angry, half-humorous twinkle in his eyes, glanced at it.

"If this is your Barnsdale teaching," he rejoined, "it is the teaching of cowards. Here you are, with a bow in your hands, ready to shoot a man who has only his walking staff for a weapon."

Robin paused. He was downright angry with the stranger, but there was something honest and good-natured about the giant which he liked.

"Have it your way, then," he said. "Wait here." He turned and went back to the bank, where he cut a stout staff of his own, and trimmed it to the weight and length he desired. Then he jumped back onto the bridge.

"Now," said Robin, "we will play a little game together. Whoever is knocked from the bridge into the stream shall lose the battle. Ready? Go!"

With the first twirl of Robin's staff, the huge stranger could see he had no novice to deal with, and he soon found that Robin's arm had strength equal to his own. For a long time their staffs whirled like the arms of two windmills, and when they clashed, the crack of wood was tossed to and fro between the trees on either side of the stream. The stranger lunged, and his stick came down with a sharp rap on Robin's skull.

"First hit goes to you!" cried Robin.

"Second hit to you!" said the giant with a good-natured laugh, rubbing a new bruise on his left forearm.

Quick as lightning the blows descended now, and the very bones of both men rattled. Keeping their footing on the narrow bridge was almost impossible. Every step made forward or backward had to be taken with great care, and the power of every blow they gave or received almost threw them over the side.

Suddenly, Robin landed a blow on the big man's crown, but the next instant, with a furious stroke, the stranger struck Robin off his balance. With a mighty splash the outlaw landed in the water.

For a moment the giant man seemed surprised to find no enemy before him. Wiping the sweat from his eyes, he cried, "Hello, good laddie, where have you gone?"

He bent down anxiously, and peered into the water flowing rapidly beneath the bridge. "By Saint Peter," he said, "I hope the bold man is not hurt!"

"Faith!" came a voice from the bank a little farther down. "Here I am, big fellow, as right as rain. You have the day, and I shall not need to cross the bridge."

Robin pulled himself up the bank and, kneeling down, washed his face in the water. When he rose, he found the big stranger at his side, dashing water over his own head.

"What?" cried Robin. "Have you not gone forward on your journey? You were in such a hurry to cross that bridge, and now you've come back!"

"Scorn me not, good fellow," said the big man. "I have nowhere to go that I know of. I am but a serf who has run away from his manor, and tonight, instead of my warm hut, I shall have only a bush to sleep under. But I would like to shake hands with you before I go, for you are as true and good a fighter as I've ever met."

Robin's hand was on the other's at once, and they gave a shake of mutual respect and liking.

"Stay awhile," said Robin. "Perhaps you would like supper before you go wandering."

With these words, Robin placed his horn to his lips and blew a blast that woke the echoes, made the blackbirds fly shrieking away, and every animal in the forest dive for the nearest cover. Then came sounds as if deer were hurrying through the bushes, and in a moment the forms of men emerged from the dark wall of trees.

"Why, good Robin," one called, "what happened to you? You're soaked to the skin!"

"'Tis no matter at all," laughed Robin. "You see that tall lad there. We fought on the bridge with our staffs, and he tumbled me in."

"Seize him, lads!" Robin's men cried, springing toward the stranger. "Toss him in and duck him well!"

"Nay, nay," shouted Robin, laughing. "Hold back, lads. I have no ill will, for he's a good fellow and bold. Listen here, my man," he said to the stranger. "We are outlaws, brave lads who hide here in the forest from the evil lords, and we make it our business to take from the rich what they've stolen from the poor. Join us if you will. I can promise both hard knocks and good cheer."

"By earth and water, I'll be your man," cried the stranger, seizing Robin's hand. "Never heard I sweeter words than those you've said, and with all my heart will I serve you and your fellowship."

"What is your name, good man?" asked Robin.

"John o' the Stubbs," replied the other, and then with a great laugh, "but men call me John the Little."

The others laughed, too, and pressed forward to shake hands with him. Then they raced back to camp, where a great iron pot waited for them over a fire, from which rose most appetizing odors for men grown hungry in greenwood air. Standing around John the Little, who overtopped them all, the outlaws held their mugs to a great wooden cask to be filled to the brim with brown ale.

"Now, lads," cried Robin, "we will baptize our new comrade into our good free company of forest lads. He has until now been called John the Little, and a sweet pretty babe he is. But from now on, he shall be called Little John. Three cheers, lads, for Little John!"

How they made the twilight ring! The leaves overhead quivered with their shouts! Then they tossed off their mugs of ale, and gathering around the caldron, they dipped their bowls into the rich stew and fell to feasting.

How the Ostrich Got His Long Neck

AFRICAN FOLKTALE

This story from Africa reminds us that choosing the wrong friends against good advice can mean big trouble.

Long ago Ostrich had a short neck, just like all the other birds. In those days Ostrich wanted more than anything to be friends with Crocodile. All the other birds warned Ostrich he was making a mistake.

"You can't trust Crocodile," Monkey said. "He's mean, and has no manners, and scares all the other animals away from the river."

"He's lazy, too," Wildebeest warned. "All he does is lie around all day, basking in the sun and waiting for dinner."

"And he thinks only of himself," Elephant added. "He'll snap at you as soon as you turn your back. No, Crocodile can't be trusted."

81

But Ostrich paid no attention at all and insisted on playing with Crocodile.

One day Crocodile was quite hungry, for he had skipped breakfast that very morning. So he said to Ostrich: "My good friend, I have a terrible toothache today. Would you mind sticking your head into my mouth and seeing what's wrong with me?"

He opened his jaws wide, very wide.

"Why, of course, dear Crocodile," Ostrich said.

And he stuck his head inside.

"But you have so many teeth!" Ostrich called. "Which is the one that aches?"

"It's one in the back," Crocodile moaned. "Look in the back!"

So Ostrich stuck his head in further.

"It's awfully dark in here," he called out again. "And so many teeth! I'm still not sure which one aches."

"It's in the very, very back," Crocodile assured him. "Go back just a little more."

So Ostrich stuck his head in even further.

"Here?" he called.

"There!" Crocodile shouted. And he snapped his jaws shut on poor Ostrich's head!

"Help!" Ostrich yelled, and he pulled as hard as he could to get his head out. But Crocodile pulled right back.

They both pulled, and they pulled. Ostrich pulled one way, and Crocodile pulled the other. And as they pulled, Ostrich's neck began to stretch.

And s–t–r–e–t–c–h.

And S—T—R—E—T—C—H!

They pulled all day long, and Ostrich's neck grew longer and longer. It must have hurt quite a bit, but Ostrich kept pulling all the same, because of course he did not want to lose his head.

At last Crocodile got tired of pulling and let go. Ostrich jumped back and ran away from the river as fast as he could. And to this day he has a long neck to remind him to stay away from the likes of Crocodile.

Jonathan and David

RETOLD BY JESSE LYMAN HURLBUT

Sometimes the duties of friendship compete with other obligations and affections. The story of Jonathan, told in the first book of Samuel in the Bible, is one such instance. Jonathan was the eldest son and heir of King Saul of Israel. He was also David's sworn friend. After David killed Goliath, Saul grew jealous of his popularity and, fearing that he would eventually become king, sought to murder him. Jonathan's defense of David, made doubly painful because of his filial duties and his own claim to the throne, is one of our greatest examples of loyalty in friendship.

After David had slain the giant, he was brought before King Saul, still holding the giant's head. Saul did not remember in this bold fighting man the boy who a few years before had played in his presence. He took him into his own house and made him an officer among his soldiers. David was as wise and as brave in the army as he had been when facing the giant, and very soon he was in command of a thousand men. All the men loved him, both in Saul's court and in his camp, for David had the spirit that drew all hearts toward him.

When David was returning from his battle with the Philistines, the women of Israel came to meet him out of the cities, with instruments of music, singing, and dancing, and they sang:

> "Saul has slain his thousands,
> And David his ten thousands."

This made Saul very angry, for he was jealous and suspicious in his spirit. He thought constantly of Samuel's words, that God would take the kingdom from him and would give it to one who was more worthy of it. He began to think that perhaps this young man, who had come in a single day to greatness before the people, might try to make himself king.

His former feeling of unhappiness again came over Saul. He raved in his house, talking as a man talks who is crazed. By this time they all knew that David was a musician, and they called him again to play on his harp and to sing before the troubled king. But now, in his madness, Saul would not listen to David's voice. Twice he threw his spear at him, but each time David leaped aside, and the spear went into the wall of the house.

Saul was afraid of David, for he saw that the Lord was with David, as the Lord was no longer with himself. He would have killed David, but did not dare kill him, because everybody loved David. Saul said to himself, "Though I cannot kill him myself, I will have him killed by the Philistines."

He sent David out on dangerous errands of war, but David came home in safety, all the greater and the more beloved after each victory. Saul said, "I will give you my daughter Merab for your wife if you will fight the Philistines for me."

David fought the Philistines; but when he came home from the war he found that Merab, who had been promised to him, had been given as wife to another man. Saul had another daughter, named Michal. She loved David and showed her love for him. Then Saul sent word to David, saying, "You shall have Michal, my daughter, for your wife when you have killed a hundred Philistines."

Then David went out and fought the Philistines, and killed two hundred of them, and they brought the word to Saul. Then Saul gave him his daughter Michal as his wife, but he was all the more afraid of David as he saw him growing in power and drawing nearer to the throne of the kingdom.

But if Saul hated David, Saul's son Jonathan saw David's courage, and the soul of Jonathan was knit to the soul of David, and Jonathan loved him as his own soul. He took off his own royal robe, and his sword, and his bow, and gave them all to David. It grieved Jonathan greatly that his father, Saul, was so jealous of David. He spoke to his father, and said: "Let not the king do harm to David; for David has been faithful to the king, and he has done great things for the kingdom. He took his life in his hand, and killed the Philistine, and won a great victory for the Lord and for the people. Why should you seek to kill an innocent man?"

For the time Saul listened to Jonathan and said, "As the Lord lives, David shall not be put to death."

And again David sat at the king's table, among the princes; and when Saul was troubled again David played on his harp and sang before him. But once more Saul's jealous anger arose, and he threw his spear at David. David was watchful and quick. He leaped aside, and, as before, the spear fastened into the wall.

Saul sent men to David's house to seize him, but Michal, Saul's daughter, who was David's wife, let David down out of the window, so that he escaped. She placed an image on David's bed and covered it with the bedclothes. When the men came, she said, "David is ill in the bed and cannot go."

They brought the word to Saul, and he said, "Bring him to me in the bed, just as he is."

When the image was found in David's bed, David was in a safe place, far away. David went to Samuel at Ramah and stayed with him among the men who were prophets worshiping God and singing and speaking God's word. Saul heard that David was there, and sent men to take him. But when these men came and saw Samuel and the prophets praising God and praying, the same spirit came on them, and they began to praise and to pray. Saul sent other men, but these also, when they came among the prophets, felt the same power and joined in the worship.

Finally Saul said, "If no other man will bring David to me, I will go myself and take him."

And Saul went to Ramah, but when he came near to the company of the worshipers, praising God, and praying, and preaching, the same spirit came on Saul. He, too, began to join in the songs and the prayers, and stayed there all that day and that night, worshiping God very earnestly. When the next day he went again to his home in Gibeah, his feeling was changed for the time, and he was again friendly to David.

But David knew that Saul was at heart his bitter enemy and would kill him if he could as soon as his madness came upon him. He met Jonathan out in the field away from the place. Jonathan said to David:

"Stay away from the king's table for a few days, and I will find out how he feels toward you and will tell you. Perhaps even now my father may become your friend. But if he is to be your enemy, I know that the Lord is with you, and that Saul will not succeed against you. Promise me that as long as you live you will be kind to me, and not only to me while I live but to my children after me."

Jonathan believed, as many others believed, that David would yet become the king of Israel, and he was willing to give up to David his right to be king, such was his great love for him. That day a promise was made between Jonathan and David, that they and their children, and those who should come after them, should be friends forever.

Jonathan said to David, "I will find how my father feels toward you and will bring you word. After three days I will be here with my bow and arrows, and I will send a little boy out near your place of hiding, and I will shoot three arrows. If I say to the boy, 'Run, find the arrows, they are on this side of you,' then you can come safely, for the king will not harm you. But if I call out to the boy, 'The arrows are away beyond you,' that will mean that there is danger, and you must hide from the king."

So David stayed away from Saul's table for two days. At first Saul said nothing of his absence, but at last he said:

"Why has not the son of Jesse come to meals yesterday and today?"

And Jonathan said, "David asked leave of me to go to his home at Bethlehem and visit his oldest brother."

Then Saul was very angry. He cried out, "You are a disobedient son! Why have you chosen this enemy of mine as your best friend? Do you not know that as long as he is alive you can never be king? Send after him, and let him be brought to me, for he shall surely die!"

Saul was so fierce in his anger that he threw his spear at his own son Jonathan. Jonathan rose up from the table, so anxious for his friend David that he could eat nothing. The next day, at the hour agreed upon, Jonathan went out into the field with a little boy. He said to the boy, "Run out yonder, and be ready to find the arrows that I shoot."

And as the boy was running Jonathan shot arrows beyond him, and he called out, "The arrows are away beyond you; run quickly and find them."

The boy ran and found the arrows and brought them to Jonathan. He gave the bow and arrows to the boy, saying to him, "Take them back to the city. I will stay here awhile."

And as soon as the boy was out of sight David came from his hiding place and ran to Jonathan. They fell into each other's arms and kissed each other again and again, and wept together. For David knew now that he must no longer hope to be safe in Saul's hands. He must leave home, and wife, and friends, and his father's house, and hide wherever he could from the hate of King Saul.

Jonathan said to him, "Go in peace; for we have sworn together saying, 'The Lord shall be between you and me and between your children and my children forever.'"

Then Jonathan went again to his father's palace, and David went out to find a hiding place.

Judas and Peter

TRADITIONAL

Here, from the Gospel according to Matthew, is one of our greatest stories of betrayal. We are horrified most, of course, by what Judas Iscariot did for thirty pieces of silver. At the same time, though, we are stunned in a completely different way by Peter's failure. Despite his vow at the Mount of Olives ("I will not deny thee"), Peter, in fear and misery, commits a much more forgivable, more human kind of betrayal. Judas Iscariot's treachery seems beyond comprehension, while Peter's denial is on a scale of which we are all capable.

Then one of the twelve, called Judas Iscariot, went unto the chief priests,

And said unto them, What will ye give me, and I will deliver him unto you? And they covenanted with him for thirty pieces of silver.

And from that time he sought opportunity to betray him.

Now the first day of the feast of Unleavened Bread the disciples came to Jesus, saying unto him, Where wilt thou that we prepare for thee to eat the Passover?

And he said, Go into the city to such a man, and say unto him, The Master saith, My time is at hand; I will keep the Passover at thy house with my disciples.

And the disciples did as Jesus had appointed them; and they made ready the Passover.

Now when the even was come, he sat down with the twelve.

And as they did eat, he said, Verily I say unto you, that one of you shall betray me.

And they were exceeding sorrowful, and began every one of them to say unto him, Lord, is it I?

And he answered and said, He that dippeth his hand with me in the dish, the same shall betray me.

The Son of Man goeth as it is written of him: but woe unto that man by whom the Son of Man is betrayed! it had been good for that man if he had not been born.

Then Judas, which betrayed him, answered and said, Master, is it I? He said unto him, Thou hast said.

And as they were eating, Jesus took bread, and blessed it, and brake it, and gave it to the disciples, and said, Take, eat; this is my body.

And he took the cup, and gave thanks, and gave it to them, saying, Drink ye all of it;

For this is my blood of the new testament, which is shed for many for the remission of sins.

But I say unto you, I will not drink henceforth of this fruit of the vine, until that day when I drink it new with you in my Father's kingdom.

And when they had sung a hymn, they went out into the Mount of Olives.

Then saith Jesus unto them, All ye shall be offended because of me this night: for it is written, I will smite the shepherd, and the sheep of the flock shall be scattered abroad.

But after I am risen again, I will go before you into Galilee.

Peter answered and said unto him, Though all men shall be offended because of thee, yet will I never be offended.

Jesus said unto him, Verily I say unto thee, That this night, before the cock crow, thou shalt deny me thrice.

Peter said unto him, Though I should die with thee, yet will I not deny thee. Likewise also said all the disciples.

Then cometh Jesus with them unto a place called Gethsemane, and saith unto the disciples, Sit ye here, while I go and pray yonder.

And he took with him Peter and the two sons of Zebedee, and began to be sorrowful and very heavy.

Then saith he unto them, My soul is exceeding sorrowful, even unto death: tarry ye here, and watch with me.

And he went a little further, and fell on his face, and prayed, saying, O my Father, if it be possible, let this cup pass from me: nevertheless, not as I will, but as thou wilt.

And he cometh unto the disciples, and findeth them asleep, and saith unto Peter, What, could ye not watch with me one hour?

Watch and pray, that ye enter not into temptation: the spirit indeed is willing, but the flesh is weak.

He went away again the second time, and prayed, saying, O my Father, if this cup may not pass away from me, except I drink it, thy will be done.

And he came and found them asleep again: for their eyes were heavy.

And he left them, and went away again, and prayed the third time, saying the same words.

Then cometh he to his disciples, and saith unto them, Sleep on now, and take your rest: behold, the hour is at hand, and the Son of Man is betrayed into the hands of sinners.

Rise, let us be going: behold, he is at hand that doth betray me.

And while he yet spake, lo, Judas, one of the twelve, came, and with him a great multitude with swords and staves, from the chief priests and elders of the people.

Now he that betrayed him gave them a sign, saying, Whomsoever I shall kiss, that same is he; hold him fast.

And forthwith he came to Jesus, and said, Hail, Master; and kissed him.

And Jesus said unto him, Friend, wherefore art thou come? Then came they, and laid hands on Jesus, and took him.

And, behold, one of them which were with Jesus stretched out his hand, and drew his sword, and struck a servant of the high priest, and smote off his ear.

Then said Jesus unto him, Put up again thy sword into his place: for all they that take the sword shall perish with the sword.

Thinkest thou that I cannot now pray to my Father, and he shall presently give me more than twelve legions of angels?

But how then shall the Scriptures be fulfilled, that thus it must be?

In that same hour said Jesus to the multitudes, Are ye come out as against a thief with swords and staves for to take me? I sat daily with you teaching in the temple, and ye laid no hold on me.

But all this was done, that the Scriptures of the prophets might be fulfilled. Then all the disciples forsook him, and fled.

And they that had laid hold on Jesus led him away to Caiaphas the high priest, where the scribes and the elders were assembled.

But Peter followed him afar off unto the high priest's palace, and went in, and sat with the servants, to see the end.

Now the chief priests, and elders, and all the council, sought false witness against Jesus, to put him to death;

But found none: yea, though many false witnesses came, yet found they none. At the last came two false witnesses,

And said, This fellow said, I am able to destroy the temple of God, and to build it in three days.

And the high priest arose, and said unto him, Answerest thou nothing? What is it which these witness against thee?

But Jesus held his peace. And the high priest answered and said unto him, I adjure thee by the living God, that thou tell us whether thou be the Christ, the Son of God.

Jesus saith unto him, Thou hast said: nevertheless I say unto you, Hereafter shall ye see the Son of Man sitting on the right hand of power, and coming in the clouds of heaven.

Then the high priest rent his clothes, saying, He hath spoken blasphemy; what further need have we of witnesses? Behold, now ye have heard his blasphemy.

What think ye? They answered and said, He is guilty of death.

Then did they spit in his face, and buffeted him; and others smote him with the palms of their hands,

Saying, Prophesy unto us, thou Christ, Who is he that smote thee?

Now Peter sat without in the palace: and a damsel came unto him, saying, Thou also wast with Jesus of Galilee.

But he denied before them all, saying, I know not what thou sayest.

And when he was gone out into the porch, another maid saw him, and said unto them that were there, This fellow was also with Jesus of Nazareth.

And again he denied with an oath, I do not know the man.

And after a while came unto him they that stood by, and said to Peter, Surely thou also art one of them; for thy speech bewrayeth thee.

Then began he to curse and to swear, saying, I know not the man. And immediately the cock crew.

And Peter remembered the word of Jesus, which said unto him, Before the cock crow, thou shalt deny me thrice. And he went out, and wept bitterly.

When the morning was come, all the chief priests and elders of the people took counsel against Jesus to put him to death:

And when they had bound him, they led him away, and delivered him to Pontius Pilate the governor.

Then Judas, which had betrayed him, when he saw that he

was condemned, repented himself, and brought again the thirty pieces of silver to the chief priests and elders,

Saying, I have sinned in that I have betrayed the innocent blood. And they said, What is that to us? See thou to that.

And he cast down the pieces of silver in the temple, and departed, and went and hanged himself.

Little Girls Wiser Than Men

LEO TOLSTOY

All friendships have their ups and downs. Learning to put aside disagreements makes companionship long-lasting.

I t was an early Easter. Sledging was only just over; snow still lay in the yards, and water ran in streams down the village street.

Two little girls from different houses happened to meet in a lane between two homesteads, where the dirty water after running through the farmyards had formed a large puddle. One girl was very small, the other a little bigger. Their mothers had dressed them both in new frocks. The little one wore a blue frock, the other a yellow print, and both had red kerchiefs on their heads. They had just come from church when they met, and first they showed each other their finery, and then they began to play. Soon the fancy took them to splash about in the water, and the smaller one was going to step into the puddle, shoes and all, when the elder checked her.

"Don't go in so, Malaaasha," said she. "Your mother will scold you. I will take off my shoes and stockings, and you take off yours."

They did so, and then, picking up their skirts, began walking toward each other through the puddle. The water came up to Malaaasha's ankles, and she said:

"It is deep, Akouaalya. I'm afraid!"

"Come on," replied the other. "Don't be frightened. It won't get any deeper."

When they got near one another, Akouaalya said:

"Mind, Malaaasha, don't splash. Walk carefully!"

She had hardly said this, when Malaaasha plumped down her foot so that the water splashed right on to Akouaalya's frock. The frock was splashed, and so were Akouaalya's eyes and nose. When she saw the stains on her frock, she was angry and ran after Malaaasha to strike her. Malaaasha was frightened, and seeing that she had got herself into trouble, she scrambled out of the puddle, and prepared to run home. Just then Akouaalya's mother happened to be passing, and seeing that her daughter's skirt was splashed, and her sleeves dirty, she said:

"You naughty, dirty girl, what have you been doing!"

"Malaaasha did it on purpose," replied the girl.

At this Akouaalya's mother seized Malaaasha, and struck her on the back of her neck. Malaaasha began to howl so that she could be heard all down the street. Her mother came out.

"What are you beating my girl for?" said she, and began scolding her neighbor. One word led to another and they had an angry quarrel. The men came out, and a crowd collected in the street, everyone shouting and no one listening. They all went on quarreling, till one gave another a push, and the affair had very nearly come to blows, when Akouaalya's old grandmother, stepping in among them, tried to calm them.

"What are you thinking of, friends? Is it right to behave so? On a day like this, too! It is a time for rejoicing, and not for such folly as this."

They would not listen to the old woman, and nearly knocked her off her feet. And she would not have been able to quiet the crowd, if it had not been for Akouaalya and Malaaasha themselves. While the women were abusing each other, Akouaalya had wiped the mud off her frock, and gone back to the puddle. She took a stone and began scraping away the earth in front of the puddle to make a channel through which the water could run out into the street. Presently Malaaasha joined her, and with a chip of wood helped her dig the channel. Just as the men were beginning to fight, the water from the little girls' channel ran streaming into the street toward the very place where the old woman was trying to pacify the men. The girls followed it, one running on each side of the little stream.

"Catch it, Malaaasha! Catch it!" shouted Akouaalya, while Malaaasha could not speak for laughing.

Highly delighted, and watching the chip float along on their stream, the little girls ran straight into the group of men; and the old woman, seeing them, said to the men:

"Are you not ashamed of yourselves? To go fighting on account of these lassies, when they themselves have forgotten all about it, and are playing happily together. Dear little souls! They are wiser than you!"

The men looked at the little girls, and were ashamed, and, laughing at themselves, went back each to his own home.

"Except ye turn, and become as little children, ye shall in no wise enter into the kingdom of heaven."

Mending Wall

ROBERT FROST

We want to make sure we don't fall into the habit of walling friend-ships in or out.

Something there is that doesn't love a wall,
That sends the frozen-ground-swell under it,
And spills the upper boulders in the sun;
And makes gaps even two can pass abreast.
The work of hunters is another thing:
I have come after them and made repair
Where they have left not one stone on a stone,
But they would have the rabbit out of hiding,
To please the yelping dogs. The gaps I mean,
No one has seen them made or heard them made,
But at spring mending-time we find them there.
I let my neighbor know beyond the hill;
And on a day we meet to walk the line

And set the wall between us once again.
We keep the wall between us as we go.
To each the boulders that have fallen to each.
And some are loaves and some so nearly balls
We have to use a spell to make them balance:
"Stay where you are until our backs are turned!"
We wear our fingers rough with handling them.
Oh, just another kind of outdoor game,
One on a side. It comes to little more:
There where it is we do not need the wall:
He is all pine and I am apple orchard.
My apple trees will never get across
And eat the cones under his pines, I tell him.
He only says, "Good fences make good neighbors."
Spring is the mischief in me, and I wonder
If I could put a notion in his head:
"*Why* do they make good neighbors? Isn't it
Where there are cows? But here there are no cows.
Before I built a wall I'd ask to know
What I was walling in or walling out,
And to whom I was like to give offense.
Something there is that doesn't love a wall,
That wants it down." I could say "Elves" to him,
But it's not elves exactly, and I'd rather
He said it for himself. I see him there
Bringing a stone grasped firmly by the top
In each hand, like an old-stone savage armed.
He moves in darkness as it seems to me,

Not of woods only and the shade of trees.
He will not go behind his father's saying,
And he likes having thought of it so well
He says again, "Good fences make good neighbors."

Penelope's Web

ADAPTED FROM JAMES BALDWIN

Penelope's long wait for her husband's return from the Trojan War may be our ultimate tale of fidelity. The Ithacan queen's patience, resourcefulness, constancy, and love make her one of Greek mythology's most memorable characters. The story comes from Homer's Odyssey. *In this retelling, Odysseus is called by his Latin name, Ulysses.*

Of all the heroes who fought against Troy, the wisest and shrewdest was Ulysses, king of Ithaca. Yet, he went unwillingly to war. He longed to stay at home with his wife, Penelope, and their baby boy, Telemachus. But the princes of Greece demanded that he help them, and at last he consented.

"Go, Ulysses," said Penelope, "and I will keep your home and kingdom safe until you return."

"Do your duty, Ulysses," said his old father, Laertes. "Go, and may wise Athena speed your coming back."

And so, bidding farewell to Ithaca and all he held dear, he sailed away to the Trojan War.

Ten long years passed, and then news reached Ithaca that the weary siege of Troy was ended, the city lay in ashes, and the Greek kings were returning to their native lands. One by one, all the heroes reached their homes, but of Ulysses and his companions there came no word. Every day, Penelope and young Telemachus and feeble old Laertes stood by the shore and gazed with aching eyes far over the waves. But no sign of sail or glinting oars could they discern. Months passed by, and then years, and still no word.

"His ships are wrecked, and he lies at the bottom of the sea," sighed old Laertes, and after that he shut himself up in his narrow room and went no more to the shore.

But Penelope still hoped and hoped. "He is not dead," she said. "And until he comes home, I will hold this fair kingdom for him."

Every day his seat was placed for him at the table. His coat was hung by his chair, his chamber was dusted, and his great bow that hung in the hall was polished.

Ten more years passed with constant watching. Telemachus became a tall, gentle-mannered young man. And throughout all Greece, men began to talk of nothing but Penelope's great nobility and beauty.

"How foolish of her," the Greek princes and chiefs said, "to be forever looking for Ulysses. Everyone knows he is dead. She ought to marry one of us now."

So one after another, the chiefs and princes who were looking for wives sailed to Ithaca, hoping to win Penelope's love. They were haughty and overbearing fellows, glorying in their own importance and wealth. Straight to the palace they went, not waiting for an invitation, for they knew they would be treated as honored guests, whether they were welcome or not.

"Come now, Penelope," they said, "we all know Ulysses is dead. We have come as suitors for your hand, and you dare not turn us away. Choose one of us, and the rest will depart."

But Penelope answered sadly, "Princes and heroes, this cannot be. I am quite sure Ulysses lives, and I must hold his kingdom for him till he returns."

"Return he never will," said the suitors. "Make your choice now."

"Give me a month longer to wait for him," she pleaded. "In my loom I have a half-finished web of soft linen. I am weaving it for the shroud of our father, Laertes, who is very old and cannot live much longer. If Ulysses fails to return by the time this web is finished, then I will choose, though unwillingly."

The suitors agreed, and made themselves at home in the palace. They seized the best of everything. They feasted daily in the great dining hall, wasting much, and helped themselves to all the wine in the cellar. They were rude and uproarious in the once quiet chambers of the palace, and insulting to the people of Ithaca.

Every day Penelope sat at her loom and wove. "See how much I have added to the length of the web?" she would say when evening came. But at night, when the suitors were asleep, she raveled out all the threads she had woven during the day. Thus although she was always at work, the web was never finished.

As the weeks passed, however, the suitors began to grow weary of waiting.

"When will that web be finished?" they impatiently asked.

"I am busy with it every day," Penelope answered, "but it grows very slowly. Such a delicate piece of work cannot be completed so quickly."

But one of the suitors, a man named Agelaus, was not satisfied. That night he crept quietly through the palace and peeped into the weaving room. There he saw Penelope busily unravelling the web by the light of a little lamp, while she whispered to herself the name of Ulysses.

The next morning the secret was known to every one of the unwelcome guests. "Fair queen," they said, "you are very cunning, but we have found you out. That web must be finished before the sun rises again, and then tomorrow you must make your choice. We shall wait no longer."

The following afternoon the unwelcome guests assembled in the great hall. The feast was set, and they ate and drank and sang and shouted as never before. They made such an uproar that the very timbers of the palace shook.

While the turmoil was at its height, Telemachus came in, followed by Eumaeus, his father's oldest and most faithful servant. Together they began to remove all the shields and swords that hung on the walls and rattled from so much commotion.

"What are you doing with those weapons?" shouted the suitors, who finally noticed the old man and the youth.

"They are becoming tarnished with smoke and dust," said Eumaeus, "and will keep much better in the treasure room."

"But we will leave my father's great bow that hangs at the head of the hall," added Telemachus. "My mother polishes it every day, and she would sadly miss it if it were removed."

"She won't be polishing it much longer," the suitors laughed. "Before this day is over, Ithaca will have a new king."

At that moment a strange beggar entered the courtyard. His feet were bare, his head was uncovered, his clothes were in rags. He approached the kitchen door, where an old greyhound, Argos, was lying on a heap of ashes. Twenty years before, Argos had been Ulysses' favorite and most loyal hunting dog. But now, grown toothless and almost blind, he was only abused by the suitors.

When he saw the beggar slowly moving through the yard, he raised his head to look. Then a strange look came suddenly into his old eyes. His tail wagged feebly, and he tried with all his failing strength to rise. He looked up lovingly into the beggar's face, and uttered a long but joyful howl like that which he once uttered in his youth when greeting his master.

The beggar stooped and patted his head. "Argos, old friend," he whispered.

The dog staggered to his feet, then fell, and was dead with the look of joy still in his eyes.

A moment later the beggar stood in the doorway of the great hall, where he was seen whispering a few words to Telemachus and faithful Eumaeus.

"What do you want here, Old Rags?" the suitors called, hurling crusts of bread at his head. "Get out! Be gone!"

But at that moment, down the stairs came Penelope, stately and beautiful, with her servants and maids around her.

"The queen! The queen!" cried the suitors. "She has come to choose one of us!"

"Telemachus, my son," said Penelope, "what poor man is this whom our guests treat so roughly?"

"Mother, he is a wandering beggar whom the waves cast upon our shores last night," answered the prince. "He says that he brings news of my father."

"Then he shall tell me of it," said the queen. "But first he must rest." At this she caused the beggar to be led to a seat at the farther side of the room, and gave orders that he be fed and refreshed.

An old woman, who had been Ulysses' nurse when he was a child, brought a great bowl of water and towels. Kneeling on the stones before the stranger, she began to wash his feet. Suddenly she sprang back, overturning the bowl in her confusion.

"O, master! The scar!" she muttered quietly.

"Dear nurse," whispered the beggar, "you were ever discreet and wise. You know me by the old scar I have carried on my knee since boyhood. Keep well the secret, for I bide my time, and the hour of vengeance is nigh."

This man in rags was indeed Ulysses, the king. Alone in a little boat he had been cast, that very morning, upon the shore of his own island. He had made himself known to Telemachus and old Eumaeus alone, and by his orders they had removed the weapons that hung on the wall of the great hall.

Meanwhile, the suitors had gathered again around the feast table and were more boisterous than before. "Come, fair Penelope!" they shouted. "This beggar can tell his tale tomorrow. It is time for you to choose a new husband! Choose now!"

"Chiefs and princes," said Penelope, in trembling tones, "let us leave this decision to the gods. Behold, there hangs the great bow of Ulysses, which he alone was able to string. Let each of you try his strength in bending it, and I will choose the one who can shoot an arrow from it the most skillfully."

"Well said!" cried all the suitors, and they lined up to try their strength. The first took the bow in his hands, and struggled long to bend it. Then, losing patience, he threw it on the ground and strode away. "None but a giant can string a bow like that," he said.

Then, one by one, the other suitors tried their strength, but all in vain.

"Perhaps the old beggar would like to take part in this contest," one said with a sneer.

Then Ulysses in his beggar's rags rose from his seat and went with halting steps to the head of the hall. He fumbled with the great bow, gazing at its polished back and its long, well-shaped arms, stout as bars of iron. "Methinks," he said, "that in my younger days I once saw a bow like this."

"Enough! Enough!" shouted the suitors. "Get out, you old fool!"

Suddenly, a great change came over the stranger. Almost without effort, he bent the great bow and strung it. Then he rose to his full height, and even in his beggar's rags appeared every inch a king.

"Ulysses! Ulysses!" Penelope cried.

The suitors were speechless. Then, in the wildest alarm, they turned and tried to escape from the hall. But the arrows of Ulysses were swift and sure, and not one missed its mark. "Now I avenge myself upon those who have tried to destroy my home!" he cried. And thus, one after another, the lawless suitors perished.

The next day Ulysses sat in the great hall with Penelope and Telemachus and all the joyful members of the household, and he told the story of his long wanderings over the sea. And Penelope, in turn, related how she had faithfully kept the kingdom, as she had promised, though beset by insolent and wicked suitors. Then she brought from her chamber a roll of soft, white cloth of wonderful delicacy and beauty, and said, "This is the web, Ulysses. I promised that on the day of its completion I would choose a husband, and I choose you."

Ruth and Naomi

RETOLD BY JESSE LYMAN HURLBUT

The book of Ruth in the Bible is the story of a widow's courageous decision to leave Moab, her homeland, and travel to Judah with her Hebrew mother-in-law, who has lost her own husband and sons. Ruth's words to Naomi are one of the greatest statements of friendship and loyalty in all of literature: "Whither thou goest, I will go; and where thou lodgest, I will lodge: thy people shall be my people, and thy God my God: Where thou diest, will I die, and there will I be buried." In Judah, Ruth's fidelity and kindness were rewarded with the love of Boaz, and through marriage to him she became the great-grandmother of King David.

In the time of the judges in Israel, a man named Elimelech was living in the town of Bethlehem, in the tribe of Judah, about six miles south of Jerusalem. His wife's name was Naomi, and his two sons were Mahlon and Chilion. For some years the crops were poor, and food was scarce in Judah; and Elimelech, with his family, went to live in the land of Moab, which was on the east of the Dead Sea, as Judah was on the west.

There they stayed ten years, and in that time Elimelech died. His two sons married women of the country of Moab, one woman named Orpah, the other named Ruth. But the two young men also died in the land of Moab, so that Naomi and her two daughters-in-law were all left widows.

Naomi heard that God had again given good harvests and bread to the land of Judah, and she rose up to go from Moab back to her own land and her own town of Bethlehem. Her two daughters-in-law loved her and both would have gone with her, though the land of Judah was a strange land to them, for they were of the Moabite people.

Naomi said to them, "Go back, my daughters, to your own mothers' homes. May the Lord deal kindly with you, as you have been kind to your husbands and to me. May the Lord grant that each of you may yet find another husband and a happy home." Then Naomi kissed them in farewell, and the three women all wept together. The two young widows said to her, "You have been a good mother to us, and we will go with you, and live among your people."

"No, no," said Naomi. "You are young and I am old. Go back and be happy among your own people."

Then Orpah kissed Naomi and went back to her people, but Ruth would not leave her. She said, "Do not ask me to leave you, for I never will. Where you go, I will go; where you live, I will live; your people shall be my people; and your God shall be my God. Where you die, I will die, and be buried. Nothing but death itself shall part you and me."

When Naomi saw that Ruth was firm in her purpose, she ceased trying to persuade her; so the two women went on together. They walked around the Dead Sea, and crossed the river Jordan, and climbed the mountains of Judah, and came to Bethlehem.

Naomi had been absent from Bethlehem for ten years, but her friends were all glad to see her again. They said, "Is this Naomi, whom we knew years ago?" Now the name Naomi means "pleasant." And Naomi said, "Call me not Naomi; call me Mara, for the Lord has made my life bitter. I went out full, with my husband and two sons; now I come home empty, without them. Do not call me 'Pleasant'; call me 'Bitter.'" The name "Mara," by which Naomi wished to be called, means "bitter." But Naomi learned later that "Pleasant" was the right name for her after all.

There was living in Bethlehem at that time a very rich man named Boaz. He owned large fields that were abundant in their harvests, and he was related to the family of Elimelech, Naomi's husband, who had died.

It was the custom in Israel when they reaped the grain not to gather all the stalks, but to leave some for the poor people, who followed after the reapers with their sickles and gathered what was left. When Naomi and Ruth came to Bethlehem, it was the time of the barley harvest, and Ruth went out into the fields to glean the grain which the reapers had left. It so happened that she was gleaning in the field that belonged to Boaz, this rich man.

Boaz came out from the town to see his men reaping, and he said to them, "The Lord be with you." They answered him, "The Lord bless you." And Boaz said to his master of the reapers, "Who is this young woman that I see gleaning in the field?"

The man answered, "It is the young woman from the land of Moab, who came with Naomi. She asked leave to glean after the reapers and has been here gathering grain since yesterday."

Then Boaz said to Ruth, "Listen to me, my daughter. Do not go to any other field, but stay here with my young women. No one shall harm you, and when you are thirsty, go and drink at our vessels of water."

Then Ruth bowed to Boaz and thanked him for his kindness, all the more kind because she was a stranger in Israel. Boaz said, "I have heard how true you have been to your mother-in-law, Naomi, in leaving your own land and coming with her to this land. May the Lord, under whose wings you have come, give you a reward!" And at noon, when they sat down to rest and to eat, Boaz gave her some of the food. And he said to the reapers, "When you are reaping, leave some of the sheaves for her, and drop out some sheaves from the bundles, where she may gather them."

That evening Ruth showed Naomi how much she had gleaned, and told her of the rich man Boaz, who had been so kind to her. And Naomi said, "This man is a near relation of ours. Stay in his fields as long as the harvest lasts." And so Ruth gleaned in the fields of Boaz until the harvest had been gathered.

At the end of the harvest, Boaz held a feast on the threshing floor. And after the feast, by the advice of Naomi, Ruth went to him, and said to him, "You are a near relation of my husband and of his father, Elimelech. Now will you not do good to us for his sake?"

And when Boaz saw Ruth he loved her, and soon after this he took her as his wife. And Naomi and Ruth went to live in his home, so that Naomi's life was no more bitter, but pleasant. And Boaz and Ruth had a son, whom they named Obed. Later Obed had a son named Jesse; and Jesse was the father of David, the shepherd boy who became king. So Ruth, the young woman of Moab, who chose the people and the God of Israel, became the mother of kings.

The Selfish Giant

OSCAR WILDE

Like the giant in this tale, we find friendship when we give something of ourselves.

Every afternoon, as they were coming from school, the children used to go and play in the Giant's garden.

It was a large, lovely garden, with soft green grass. Here and there over the grass stood beautiful flowers like stars, and there were twelve peach trees that in the springtime broke out into delicate blossoms of pink and pearl, and in the autumn bore rich fruit. The birds sat on the trees and sang so sweetly that the children used to stop their games in order to listen to them. "How happy we are here!" they cried to each other.

One day the Giant came back. He had been to visit his friend the Cornish ogre, and had stayed with him for seven years. After the seven years were over, he had said all that he had to say, for his conversation was limited, and he determined to return to his own castle. When he arrived he saw the children playing in the garden.

"What are you doing here?" he cried in a very gruff voice, and the children ran away.

"My own garden is my own garden," said the Giant. "Anyone can understand that, and I will allow nobody to play in it but myself." So he built a high wall all around it and put up a notice board.

He was a very selfish Giant.

The poor children had now nowhere to play. They tried to play on the road, but the road was very dusty and full of hard stones, and they did not like it. They used to wander round the high walls when their lessons were over and talk about the beautiful garden inside. "How happy we were there!" they said to each other.

Then the spring came, and all over the country there were little blossoms and little birds. Only in the garden of the Selfish Giant, it was still winter. The birds did not care to sing in it as there were no children, and the trees forgot to blossom. Once a beautiful flower put its head out from the grass, but when it saw the notice board, it was so sorry for the children that it slipped back into the ground again and went off to sleep. The only people who were pleased were the Snow and the Frost. "Spring has forgotten this garden," they cried, "so we will live here all the year round." The Snow covered up the grass with her great white cloak, and the Frost painted all the trees silver. Then they invited the North Wind to stay with them, and he came. He was wrapped in furs, and he roared all day about the garden, and blew the chimney pots down. "This is a delightful spot," he said. "We must ask the Hail on a visit." So the Hail came. Every day for three hours he rattled on the roof of the castle till he broke most of the slates, and then he ran round and round the garden as fast as he could go. He was dressed in gray and his breath was like ice.

"I cannot understand why the Spring is so late in coming," said the Selfish Giant, as he sat at the window and looked out at his cold, white garden. "I hope there will be a change in the weather."

But the Spring never came, nor the Summer. The Autumn gave golden fruit to every garden, but to the Giant's garden she gave none. "He is too selfish," she said. So it was always Winter there, and the North Wind and the Hail, and the Frost, and the Snow danced about through the trees.

One morning the Giant was lying awake in bed when he heard some lovely music. It sounded so sweet to his ears that he thought it must be the King's musicians passing by. It was really only a little linnet singing outside his window, but it was so long since he had heard a bird sing in his garden that it seemed to him to be the most beautiful music in the world. Then the Hail stopped dancing over his head, and the North Wind ceased roaring, and a delicious perfume came to him through the open casement. "I believe the Spring has come at last," said the Giant, and he jumped out of bed and looked out.

What did he see?

He saw a most wonderful sight. Through a little hole in the wall the children had crept in, and they were sitting in the branches of the trees. In every tree that he could see there was a little child. And the trees were so glad to have the children back again that they had covered themselves with blossoms, and were waving their arms gently above the children's heads. The birds were flying about and twittering with delight, and the flowers were looking up through the green grass and laughing. It was a lovely scene, only in one corner it was still winter. It was the farthest corner of the garden, and in it was standing a little boy. He was so small that he could not reach up to the branches of the tree, and he was wandering all around it, crying bitterly. The poor tree was still covered with frost and snow, and the North Wind was blowing and roaring above it. "Climb up! little boy," said the Tree, and it bent its branches down as low as it could; but the boy was too tiny.

And the Giant's heart melted as he looked out. "How selfish I have been!" he said. "Now I know why the Spring would not come here. I will put that poor little boy on the top of the tree, and then I will knock down the wall, and my garden shall be the children's playground for ever and ever." He was really very sorry for what he had done.

So he crept downstairs and opened the front door quite softly, and went out into the garden. But when the children saw him, they were so frightened that they all ran away, and the garden became winter again. Only the little boy did not run, for his eyes were so full of tears that he did not see the Giant coming. And the Giant stole up behind him and took him gently in his hand and put him up into the tree. And the tree broke at once into blossom, and the birds came and sang on it, and the little boy stretched out his two arms and flung them around the

Giant's neck and kissed him. And the other children, when they saw that the Giant was not wicked any longer, came running back, and with them came the Spring. "It is your garden now, little children" said the Giant, and he took a great axe and knocked down the wall. And when the people were going to market at twelve o'clock, they found the Giant playing with the children in the most beautiful garden they had ever seen.

All day long they played, and in the evening they came to the Giant to bid him goodbye.

"But where is your little companion?" he said. "The boy I put into the tree." The Giant loved him the best because he had kissed him.

"We don't know," answered the children. "He has gone away."

"You must tell him to be sure and come tomorrow," said the Giant. But the children said that they did not know where he lived and had never seen him before; and the Giant felt very sad.

Every afternoon, when school was over, the children came and played with the Giant. But the little boy whom the Giant loved was never seen again. The Giant was very kind to all the children, yet he longed for his first little friend, and often spoke of him. "How I would like to see him!" he used to say.

Years went over, and the Giant grew very old and feeble. He could not play about anymore, so he sat in a huge armchair, and watched the children at their games, and admired his garden. "I have many beautiful flowers," he said. "But the children are the most beautiful flowers of all."

One winter morning he looked out of his window as he was

dressing. He did not hate the Winter now, for he knew that it was merely the Spring asleep, and that the flowers were resting.

Suddenly he rubbed his eyes in wonder and looked and looked. It certainly was a marvelous sight. In the farthest corner of the garden was a tree quite covered with lovely white blossoms. Its branches were golden, and silver fruit hung down from them, and underneath it stood the little boy he had loved.

Downstairs ran the Giant in great joy, and out into the garden. He hastened across the grass, and came near to the child. And when he came quite close his face grew red with anger, and he said, "Who hath dared to wound thee?" For on the palms of the child's hands were the prints of two nails, and the prints of two nails were on the little feet.

"Who hath dared to wound thee?" cried the Giant. "Tell me, that I may take my big sword and slay him."

"Nay," answered the child. "But these are the wounds of Love."

"Who art thou?" said the Giant, and a strange awe fell on him, and he knelt before the little child.

And the child smiled on the Giant, and said to him, "You let me play once in your garden; today you shall come with me to my garden, which is Paradise."

And when the children ran in that afternoon, they found the Giant lying dead under the tree, all covered with white blossoms.

The Story of Cincinnatus

RETOLD BY JAMES BALDWIN

This story of Roman statesman and general Lucius Quinctius Cincinnatus takes place in 458 B.C., when Rome was besieged by an Italic tribe called the Aequi. It is one of our most famous reminders that the loyal citizen expects no great reward for coming to his country's aid. Whenever I visit Cincinnati, I try to stop by the statue of Cincinnatus there, one of my favorites.

There was a man named Cincinnatus who lived on a little farm not far from the city of Rome. He had once been rich, and had held the highest office in the land, but in one way or another he had lost all his wealth. He was now so poor that he had to do all the work on his farm with his own hands. But in those days it was thought to be a noble thing to till the soil.

Cincinnatus was so wise and just that everybody trusted him and asked his advice. When anyone was in trouble and did

124

not know what to do, his neighbors would say, "Go and tell Cincinnatus. He will help you."

Now there lived among the mountains, not far away, a tribe of fierce, half-wild men, who were at war with the Roman people. They persuaded another tribe of bold warriors to help them, and then marched toward the city, plundering and robbing as they came. They boasted that they would tear down the walls of Rome, and burn the houses, and kill all the men, and make slaves of the women and children.

At first the Romans, who were very proud and brave, did not think there was much danger. Every man in Rome was a soldier, and the army which went out to fight the robbers was the finest in the world. No one stayed at home but the white-haired "Fathers," as they were called, who made the laws for the city, and a small company of men who guarded the walls. Everybody thought that it would be an easy thing to drive the men of the mountains back to the place where they belonged.

But one morning five horsemen came riding down the road from the mountains. They rode with great speed, and both men and horses were covered with dust and blood. The watchman at the gate knew them and shouted to them as they galloped in. Why did they ride thus? And what had happened to the Roman army?

They did not answer him, but rode into the city and along the quiet streets. Everybody ran after them, eager to find out what was the matter. Rome was not a large city at that time, and soon they reached the marketplace where the white-haired Fathers were sitting. Then they leaped from their horses and told their story.

"Only yesterday," they said, "our army was marching through

a narrow valley between two steep mountains. All at once a thousand savage men sprang out from among the rocks before us and above us. They had blocked up the way, and the pass was so narrow that we could not fight. We tried to come back, but they had blocked up the way on this side of us, too. The fierce men of the mountains were before us and behind us, and they were throwing rocks down upon us from above. We had been caught in a trap. Then ten of us set spurs to our horses, and five of us forced our way through, but the other five fell before the spears of the mountain men. And now, O Roman Fathers! Send help to our army at once, or every man will be slain, and our city will be taken."

"What shall we do?" said the white-haired Fathers. "Whom can we send but the guards and the boys? And who is wise enough to lead them, and thus save Rome?"

All shook their heads and were very grave, for it seemed as if there was no hope. Then one said, "Send for Cincinnatus. He will help us."

Cincinnatus was in the field plowing when the men who had been sent to him came in great haste. He stopped and greeted them kindly, and waited for them to speak.

"Put on your cloak, Cincinnatus," they said, "and hear the words of the Roman people."

Then Cincinnatus wondered what they could mean. "Is all well with Rome?" he asked. And he called to his wife to bring him his cloak.

She brought the cloak, and Cincinnatus wiped the dust from his hands and arms and threw it over his shoulders. Then the men told their errand.

They told him how the army with all the noblest men of Rome had been entrapped in the mountain pass. They told him about the great danger the city was in. Then they said, "The people of Rome make you their ruler and the ruler of their city, to do with everything as you choose. And the Fathers bid you come at once and go out against our enemies, the fierce men of the mountains."

So Cincinnatus left his plow standing where it was and hurried to the city. When he passed through the streets and gave orders as to what should be done, some of the people were afraid, for they knew that he had all power in Rome to do what he pleased. But he armed the guards and the boys, and went out at their head to fight the fierce mountain men, and free the Roman army from the trap into which it had fallen.

A few days afterward there was great joy in Rome. There was good news from Cincinnatus. The men of the mountains had been beaten with great loss. They had been driven back into their own place.

And now the Roman army, with the boys and the guards, was coming home with banners flying and shouts of victory. And at their head rode Cincinnatus. He had saved Rome.

Cincinnatus might then have made himself king, for his word was law, and no man dared lift a finger against him. But, before the people could thank him enough for what he had done, he gave back the power to the white-haired Roman Fathers, and went again to his little farm and his plow.

He had been the ruler of Rome for sixteen days.

Thinking on Friendship

WILLIAM SHAKESPEARE

Thinking of friends and their worth is often enough to drive away an army of fears, regrets, and envies.

SONNET XXIX

When, in disgrace with fortune and men's eyes,
I all alone beweep my outcast state,
And trouble deaf heaven with my bootless cries,
And look upon myself, and curse my fate,
Wishing me like to one more rich in hope,
Featured like him, like him with friends possess'd,
Desiring this man's art and that man's scope,
With what I most enjoy contented least;
Yet in these thoughts myself almost despising,
Haply I think on thee, and then my state,
Like to the lark at break of day arising

From sullen earth, sings hymns at heaven's gate;
For thy sweet love remember'd such wealth brings
That then I scorn to change my state with kings.

SONNET XXX

When to the sessions of sweet silent thought
I summon up remembrance of things past,
I sigh the lack of many a thing I sought,
And with old woes new wail my dear time's waste:
Then can I drown an eye, unused to flow,
For precious friends hid in death's dateless night,
And weep afresh love's long since cancel'd woe,
And moan the expense of many a vanish'd sight:
Then can I grieve at grievances foregone,
And heavily from woe to woe tell o'er
The sad account of fore-bemoaned moan,
Which I new pay as if not paid before.
But if the while I think on thee, dear friend,
All losses are restored and sorrows end.

Why Frog and Snake Never Play Together

AFRICAN FOLKTALE

This African folktale makes us think about how much companionship the world has missed because people are told they "can't" be friends with each other.

Once upon a time, the child of the Frog was hopping along in the bush when he spied someone new lying across the path before him. This someone was long and slender, and his skin seemed to shine with all the colors of the rainbow.

"Hello there," called Frog-child. "What are you doing lying here in the path?"

"Just warming myself in the sun," answered the someone new, twisting and turning and uncoiling himself. "My name is Snake-child. What's yours?"

"I'm Frog-child. Would you like to play with me?"

So Frog-child and Snake-child played together all morning long in the bush.

"Watch what I can do," said Frog-child, and he hopped high into the air. "I'll teach you how, if you want," he offered.

So he taught Snake-child how to hop, and together they hopped up and down the path through the bush.

"Now watch what I can do," said Snake-child, and he crawled on his belly straight up the trunk of a tall tree. "I'll teach you if you want."

So he taught Frog-child how to slide on his belly and climb into trees.

After a while they both grew hungry and decided to go home for lunch, but they promised each other to meet again the next day.

"Thanks for teaching me how to hop," called Snake-child.

"Thanks for teaching me how to crawl up trees," called Frog-child.

Then they each went home.

"Look what I can do, Mother!" cried Frog-child, crawling on his belly.

"Where did you learn how to do that?" his mother asked.

"Snake-child taught me," he answered. "We played together in the bush this morning. He's my new friend."

"Don't you know the Snake family is a bad family?" his mother asked. "They have poison in their teeth. Don't ever let me catch you playing with one of them again. And don't let me see you crawling on your belly, either. It isn't proper."

Meanwhile, Snake-child went home and hopped up and down for his mother to see.

"Who taught you to do that?" she asked.

"Frog-child did," he said. "He's my new friend."

"What foolishness," said his mother. "Don't you know we've been on bad terms with the Frog family for longer than anyone can remember? The next time you play with Frog-child, catch him and eat him up. And stop that hopping. It isn't our custom."

So the next morning when Frog-child met Snake-child in the bush, he kept his distance.

"I'm afraid I can't go crawling with you today," he called, hopping back a hop or two.

Snake-child eyed him quietly, remembering what his mother had told him. "If he gets too close, I'll spring at him and eat him," he thought. But then he remembered how much fun they had had together, and how nice Frog-child had been to teach him how to hop. So he sighed sadly to himself and slid away into the bush.

And from that day onward, Frog-child and Snake-child never played together again. But they often sat alone in the sun, each thinking about their one day of friendship.

Acknowledgments

The editor gratefully acknowledges the endeavors of scholars and collectors such as James Baldwin and Jesse Lyman Hurlbut, who in a past age devoted their energies to preserving some of the best of our heritage, and whose works have supplied this volume with many truly great stories.

Reasonable care has been taken to trace ownership and, when necessary, obtain permission for each selection included.

Also Available from William J. Bennett

Villiam Bennett's *The Book of Virtues* and *The Moral Compass* have quickly become classics thanks to their homespun truth, traditional values, and moral ideals. Focusing on relationship, leadership, and courage—traits often lost in today's self-centered, cynical society—this collection of favorite stories, anecdotes, and legends reminds us of virtues of yesterday that can still be moral beacons for us today.

W PUBLISHING GROUP™
www.wpublishinggroup.com